Dedicated to:

Irene Grandison Clark and Joan Lawson
for their work in creating the National
Branch of the Imperial Society of Teachers
of Dancing

Acknowledgements
The authors would like to extend their grateful thanks for the help, advice
and criticism given on the various countries from the following:
Arni Bjornsson, Frank and Doreen Cook, Sandra Dahlqvist, Harry Goss,
Elas E Guojonsson, Nigel and Margaret Allenby-Jaffe, Halldor J Jonsson,
Hedda Klingerova-Jolly, Richard Muncey, Roderyk Lange, Phrosso Pfister,
Peter Siptar, Cesara Tiratelli, Ken Ward, June Wilson.
Also to the Austrian Institute, and the Royal Danish Embassy.
A particular thank you is given to David Leonard of Dance Books for his
help and understanding in presenting this book.

ii

Aspects of Folk Dance in Europe

Helen Wingrave & Robert Harrold

∽

DANCE BOOKS
Cecil Court, London WC2

First published in 1984 by
Dance Books Ltd.,
15 Cecil Court, London WC2N 4EZ

ISBN 0 903102 79 X

Printed by
MPG Books Ltd,
Victoria Square,
Bodmin,
Cornwall PL31 1EG

Contents

INTRODUCTION

During the past years there has been a tremendous growth of interest throughout the world in the folk arts: dance, music, song and crafts. There are now numerous folk festivals, state companies, folk societies, magazines, as well as performing groups, clubs and classes. In the field of education, folk dance holds an important place, not only in creating an interest and understanding between cultures and nations but for the physical, psychological and social values that it contains.

Folk dancing is an activity which can be experienced and shared at all levels, and for all age groups, hence its popularity, recognition and appraisal. It is a form of movement that can be introduced at all levels; to the very young, through to the older or senior age group or people with disabilities. Most people dance purely for enjoyment and for the knowledge and background that is contained within the dances. There are many dancers who rise to the challenge of examinations and tests, others work towards leadership and teaching qualifications, in which an understanding of style, music, costume etc., is essential.

Numerous books have been written (many in the language of the country) on all aspects of folk dance: music, costumes, customs etc., each subject being a complete study on its own. Dance specialists have made studies of one particular region or style, the subject being a vast and never-ending one of research and learning. In this book only an outline is given to enable the dancer, student or teacher to appreciate more fully the wealth and heritage contained in folk dance and so heighten the enjoyment of the dance.

For teachers who are interested in choreography or adapting folk material for the stage, it is essential to have depth of knowledge on the style, patterns, steps, music, customs etc.

Dance is found in every country of the world but because of the differing stages in man's evolution and the differences in culture, climate and environment, each society has developed, adapted or modified dance movement to suit their needs. Walks, runs and skips are common to most countries but people execute them in very different ways, no two countries are quite the same in style and interpretation. Each country in this book has been divided into sections giving an outline on what these differences are, and what it is that causes them. The different aspects of the background has been considered under five main headings: General Background, Music, Costume, Traditional Dances and Style, and Customs. The bibliography at the end of the book is intended to help the student who wishes to pursue the subject in more depth, but it is by no means a complete list of books available. The purpose of this book is only to indicate the various influences which affect

1

characterisation and a correct sense of style. The subject of music is the aspect most neglected by those studying folk dance, and yet music is the basis of all dance. When live or recorded music is played on the traditional instruments then dancers immediately respond and the correct style is developed. A knowledge of the different types of instruments used, the sound and quality that they produce is extremely valuable when assessing the style and the way people dance in the different countries, rather than to be too concerned with the number of beats in a bar.

To divide Europe into political boundaries is a convenient way of tabulating the different sections; but not always very accurate in assessing a style of movement. In the USSR for example, to discuss the style of Russian dancing in fact only refers to the RSFSR, the largest of the Republics (in which Moscow is situated) it will not apply to how the people dance in Moldavia or the Caucasus. In many countries there is a marked difference in movement between those who live in agricultural areas and those in the mountain regions, or even between urban and rural districts.

General Background

The geographical situation of the country, its position in Europe in relation to the surrounding countries. The type of climate and whether the country is flat, mountainous, fertile, barren, and the chief industries or occupations of the people. Whether the country has a coastline or is land-locked.

Music

The traditional form of music and the type of instruments used is the most important influence on quality in movement, in each country special reference is made to them. The form of the melodic line, which in turn has been influenced by the "sound" of the language, i.e. the strongly accented, rather boisterous rhythms of the German dances and songs reflect the spoken word of this country, or the small intervals in French music match the precise form of their speech. Harmony varies between eastern and western Europe whether sung or played on instruments.

Costume

The shape, weight and colour of costume is of great significance. The type of footwear, whether light, heavy, and how it affects the way a dancer uses the feet. The shape, weight, length or width of the women's skirts. The headdress and its influence on movement, the carriage of the body and restrictions on the use of the head.

2

Traditional Dances and Style

The form of dance and patterns, whether couples or circles, social or ritual. The type of movement and technique required to express the style of dance in a particular region, if light or heavy, staccato or flowing, precise or relaxed.

Customs

Festivals, superstitions, work themes and seasonal occupations associated with agriculture, customs derived from religious or pagan rites, reflect the character of a country or region and the people. For those interested in choreography and stage presentations a folk theme can be the basis of a group or solo.

Glossary

At the end of the book a Glossary covers some of the technical and musical terms.

To all dancers, the authors hope that they will continue to enjoy and perhaps through the pages of this book deepen and heighten their experience of folk dance, as well as developing an understanding and knowledge of other cultures, and an awareness of themselves. To teachers and leaders, we have a responsibility to those in our care, whether they be old or young and it is important that we present to them the very best. Perhaps in doing this, we are through folk dance preparing dancers to work together for a better world.

ICELAND

Interesting in pattern and music showing the influence of Denmark and Norway.

General Background

Set in the North Atlantic and under 500 miles from Scotland, Iceland is an island of wild terrain, with rivers, waterfalls, snow covered mountains, glaciers and volcanoes.

Known as the "land of fire and ice" it blends the temperate climate brought by the Gulf Stream with the cold currents of the Arctic. The island has few natural reserves but the fast-flowing rivers produce hydro-electric power and the natural steam heats the houses and public buildings and provides hot water. The capital Reykjavik means "steamy or smokey bay" after the many hot springs in this district.

The land is ideal for the rearing of sheep, there are over 800,000 and also for breeding the sturdy Icelandic ponies, direct descendants of the horses brought over by the settlers from western Norway over a thousand years ago. Other immigrants came from settlements in the British Isles, Orkney, Shetland, Scotland and Ireland, some bringing with them Celtic wives, and introducing Christianity to the island.

In the 10th Century, the first parliament or general assembly was founded which established Iceland as the first Republic in Europe and making it the world's oldest surviving administration. In the 13th Century Iceland came under the jurisdiction of Norway and later, that of Denmark. In 1944 it became an independent republic once again.

The chief industries are fishing and agriculture.

Music

Until the advent of the aeroplane, travel in Iceland was very restricted, the various farms and communities being very isolated. Wood was in very short supply and metal not available, so people, understandably relied on singing rather than making their own instruments. The melodic line was simple and a most interesting feature of the singing (usually in a two part harmony) was the interval of a 5th and known as Quintsong. The music had a sad quality and was usually sung by two men, the final notes of the phrase being sustained. Beethoven uses the interval of a 5th with great effect at the beginning of the 9th Symphony and Wagner in the Overture of the Flying

Dutchman. The interval is also found in Norwegian folk music. It was during a storm that Wagner took refuge on the Norwegian coast which influenced the writing of his opera.

Rimur or rhyme songs were also very popular, these being fast and lively. They were half spoken and half sung with the first beat of each bar being accented, and with constant changes of rhythm.

The most popular instrument was the *langspil*, a bowed zither with one string for the melody and several drones. A similar instrument is also found in Norway. The music is still mediaeval and rather solemn in style and reflects the grandeur of the Icelandic mountains and landscape, whilst the quicker music reflects the liveliness of the people, the rushing water and the sea.

Many of the songs have been collected by Bjarni Thorsteinsson.

Costume

Unlike other European countries, Icelandic national costume does not change from region to region. Wool was used extensively for clothing, being both warm and protective. Unlike other northern countries who favour bright colours, the Icelanders use black a great deal.

There are three distinct varieties of national costume for women: the festive dress, *skautbuningur*, the dress-up costume, *peysufot*, and the every-day costume, *upphlutur*. However, only very few women, all elderly, still wear national costumes as part of their ordinary dress, costumes being predominantly used on special occasions, and for folk dancing. The *upphlutur* is the most popular of the three costumes. In its present day version it consists of a black sleeveless bodice over a white long sleeved blouse, a long black skirt and an apron of various colours, frequently checked, or with lengthwise stripes. The round shallow black cap has a long black silk tassel hanging down at one side, and where it joins the cap is decorated by a silver or gilt ornamented tube. Silver or gold embroidery with stylized floral motifs decorates the front of the bodice, and around the waist a black belt is worn with a silver or gilt clasp and matching ornaments. Lately 18th and 19th century costumes (which were quite colourful) have been revived, especially for use in folk dancing.

There is no present day national costume for men. Folk dancers use the men's costume from about 1800 which corresponds with those worn by the women. It consists of a white shirt, breeches, a sleeveless waistcoat and a high cut single or double breasted jacket with many buttons, usually of silver. With it is worn a stocking cap with a short tassel, knitted stockings and sheepskin shoes.

Traditional Dances and Style

The oldest form of Icelandic dance is the circle or chain formation. These were song-dances, frequently containing interesting changes of rhythm and step patterns. A typical feature was the acting of the song which accompanied it, the words and meaning of the song forming the basis for the dance movement. The dances were mainly performed indoors at times of celebrations and as the evening progressed they became very boisterous. With the coming of the Lutheran Reformation, dance was not encouraged, and many of the old dances became lost, although several have survived. In the 19th Century, the longways and square sets which were popular in Europe and Scandinavia, also travelled to Iceland and formed the basis of many of their dances.

Customs

In common with other northern countries, there are many superstitions and customs based on Nordic mythology. The gods associated with water (the sea and rivers) and their attendant trolls and elves, are a recurring theme with counterparts in Norway and Denmark, but with slight variations. The fear of a baby being turned into a changeling was overcome by placing in the cradle a Bible open at the Gospel of St. John. Once a baby had cut its first tooth, it was considered to be safe. An iron bar was thought to ward off evil spirits and a copper hammer, representing the one used by God Thor was a magic symbol.

The most popular festivals are connected with the seasons, understandable in a country which has long, dark winters and short summers when it hardly gets dark. The First Day of Summer occurs in April and is considered second only in popularity to Christmas and New Year; special summer presents are given on this day. The prediction of the forthcoming weather is told by various rhymes associated with seeing or hearing different birds. Special Summer Day cakes were baked, these were large, flat, made of rye and had fish, meat, etc. placed on top. June is called No Night Month, there being daylight for nearly 24 hours. It is a time to gather different herbs and special stones believed to have curative and magical properties. If these were found on St. John's Day or Midsummer's Night they would be particularly beneficial. Unlike other parts of Europe and due to the lack of wood, bonfires are very uncommon on this day.

September is the month of "The Round-up of the Sheep" and in late October occurs the First Day of Winter. The winter is predicted by studying the Milky Way, by the intestines of the first sheep that is slain, and the behaviour and movement of various animals. St. Paul's Day, January 25th, was also used to predict the winter weather and extra food was put out for the ravens, the farmer hoping that if they were well fed they would stay away from the young lambs in the spring.

Festivities usually take place indoors when large quantities of food were served, consisting of smoked lamb, whale, shark, seal's flippers, dried fish, etc. One of these feasts is known as a Thorrablot, possibly a derivation of the name Thor, the god of thunder.

NORTH # NORWAY

The Norwegians are a friendly race and their dances have a lively quality — usually with an undulating action reflecting the movements and sound of water.

General Background

Scenically, the most spectacular of all the Scandinavian countries with their fjords, snow-capped mountains, dense forests, deep valleys and many lakes.

On the west the coastline is bordered by the stormy Atlantic and Arctic Oceans, and is exceptionally long due to its rugged outline, in fact 17,000 miles.

The eastern section is bordered by Sweden.

The South, where the capital Oslo is situated, is bordered by the Skager-rak; here the climate is much more temperate and having lovely beaches and good fishing.

The North extends up to the Arctic Circle and is populated by Lapps, and known as the Land of the Midnight Sun, and bordered on its north-eastern corner by Russia and Finland.

The Norwegians are a tall, fair-haired race, reflecting their Viking origin. Before 1066 they had considerable power in England and Ireland — interesting to note too that William The Conqueror was a direct descendant of their Viking King Rollo! Later they came under the dominion of Denmark and Sweden only becoming independent of the former in 1814, and Sweden in 1905. Their language today has two distinct forms showing the Danish and Swedish roots.

Fishing and forestry and now oil are the main industries and their numerous water-falls are used for hydro-electric power.

The boat in olden days being the only mode of transport, the Vikings called the sea route "the way to the north", or Norvegar and from this came the name Norway.

Music

The language of the Norwegians has rather a sing-song or lilting quality — the voice usually dropping at the end of a sentence, this often resulting in the music modulating to a minor key at the end of a phrase. Singing as an accompaniment to the folk-dance is common to many other countries in Europe; but up to the Middle Ages it was the only form in Norway.

In the 16th Century a type of harp was used called the *"langeleik"*; this was laid flat on a table and the strings plucked with a plectrum. In the 18th Century the Hardanger fiddle appeared and is still in use today. It is larger than the modern violin, has more strings and produces a strange drone-like sound.

Most of the music is written in 2/4 or 3/4 time, often with dotted notes and triplets which give it a more lively quality than that of other Scandinavian countries. Some of the 3/4 rhythms have an accented second beat, thus showing the Polish influence. The phrasing is frequently uneven, thus giving an added interest in the step sequences.

Grieg and Torgussen have given us a wonderful selection of compositions based on folk-themes.

Costume

In spite of 500 years of domination, the Norwegians have preserved their own traditions and costumes. The difficult terrain and climate kept travel to a minimum, which led to an individual development of costume in each region. During the long, dark winters, materials were woven and dyed, stockings knitted and garments embroidered. Women's skirts are full, fairly heavy and vary from calf or ankle length to the full double skirt of Setesdal. Unlike Denmark and Sweden, the Norwegians favour embroidered bodices, either on the front, sides or edges. Blouses are white and worn with most costumes. Silver and gold jewellery is very popular, the designs reflecting their Viking ancestry. Many costumes have loose pockets or bags attached to a belt by silver hooks. Headdresses are simple, and based on little caps and bonnets. Silver buckled shoes are worn with black stockings. Red, black, and white are the basic colours with green used mainly in embroidery and trimming.

The men wear black breeches tied below the knees with coloured braid. Black, red or green waistcoats are fastened with a double row of silver or gold buttons. Short jackets are also worn. White socks with black silver buckled shoes are most usual. In the past many Norwegian men became mercenaries and the dungaree type of costume from Setesdal which has leather on the trousers is thought to be based on the pattern of the uniform of the Spanish Cavalry.

Traditional Dances and Style

The dances are of three main types:

1) Those of the older tradition (usually circular) accompanied by song, the words telling of the old Norse legends and the dancers enacting the story.

2) Figure dances — many of these based on the patterns of the English and Scottish country dances.

3) Couple or pair dances — Waltzes, Rheinlanders, Polkas, Mazurkas and the Polsdanser originally from Poland and arriving in Norway via Sweden in the 17th Century.

The Halling is a dance for men only, who demonstrate their strength and agility. Another famous dance is the Springar which has many steps and quite complicated rhythms.

Cross accents are often performed by the dancers, if in 4/4 time the step taking one and a half bars of music, or in 3/4 time the dancer accenting every other beat thus giving a syncopated effect.

Customs

Christmas trees are always associated with Norway. During the second world-war, King Haakon lived in exile in London. Each year Norwegian Commandoes returned to their country on secret missions and brought back a fir-tree for their King's Christmas. The people of Oslo perpetuate this gesture every year at the festive season and we see it standing in Trafalgar Square.

A wreath made with foliage from the fir tree (or of straw) is very popular in their homes. It is hung from the ceiling and decorated with candles and ribbons.

Superstitions associated with trolls, giants, water-sprites and various evil spirits resulted in many strange practices in order to protect individuals from their spells:
   a) Putting a bowl of porridge outside the front door at night
   b) Placing mountain ash or rowan berries on the front door step
   c) Hanging a horse-shoe or piece of steel on the front door
   d) Hanging a scythe on the stable door to protect the animals
   e) Having a steel object under one's pillow at night — a knife or pair of scissors
   f) From a child's birth to the day of christening a candle always was kept alight in its room
   g) Ringing of church bells

h) Placing of shoes with heels towards the bed to prevent bad dreams caused by the visit of a "mare" (from which we have derived the term "nightmare")

The Norwegians are great craftsmen, particularly in metal and leather-work, also wood-carving and weaving.

In Western Telemark a local custom still persists, that of giving the bride on her wedding day a large brooch representing the sun. (This is very often a family heirloom).

At Easter time birch branches are carried in processing and decorated with paper streamers and called "Faselauneris". Painted eggs are very popular too — a custom found in many other countries.

The giving of flowers on every social occasion is practiced by everyone.

SWEDEN

The Swedish people dance with strong, well controlled movement.

General Background

Sweden is the largest of the Scandinavian countries and is Europe's fourth largest country after Russia, Spain and France. It is a land of forests, rivers, lakes and mountains all of which contribute to the country's three major resources, timber, hydro-electric power and iron ore. The country extends northwards for nearly 1,000 miles, well into the Arctic Circle. The total population is less than half that of London and three-quarters of the people live in the southern provinces which contain the major cities of Stockholm, Gothenburg and Malmo. Half the country is covered with forests and there are numerous lakes, two, Lake Vänern and Lake Vättern, being amongst the largest in Europe. Sweden's relatively mild climate is unique for a country so far north. The Gulf Stream, the huge ocean current which brings warm water from the West Indies to the North Atlantic, makes it possible to cultivate the forests and grow potatoes and grain.

Sweden has not always lived peacefully with the neighbouring countries and at one time Denmark, Norway and Finland all came under Swedish domination. It was in the 17th Century that Sweden became a great power when Denmark, Norway, Poland, Estonia, Latvia, the region around Leningrad and all the important coastal towns and areas on the Baltic Sea came under Swedish rule.

In 1700 the occupied countries pooled their resources and attacked the Swedish–Finnish Empire and gradually the country declined as a great power. In the latter half of the 19th Century, due to loss of employment and extreme poverty caused by the Industrial Revolution a million Swedes emigrated to North America, at one time as many as 1,000 a week.

The Swedish language belongs to the Nordic branch of the Germanic root. Swedes, Norwegians and Danes can make themselves understood. In Finland there is a Swedish-speaking minority.

Music

During the past hundred years, the revival and interest in folk-lore in this country has been considerable, therefore the music accompanying the dances is of great importance.

In olden days, wind instruments were most significant, later the violin known as the *nyckelharpa* was heard everywhere. Today the modern violin is played in conjunction with simple percussion effects and the ever popular accordion.

The music is bright and rather uncomplicated in harmony, and usually in simple time signatures; but it will be observed that if in 3/4 time and accompanying steps with the name *polska*, the emphasis will be on the second beat — this showing the Polish influence.

Costume

The basic and most popular costume worn by the women consists of a long-sleeved, high-necked white blouse over which is worn a tight-fitting bodice. The bodices can vary in shape and colour. A brightly flowered shawl is fastened at the neck or tucked into the bodice. The handspun woven skirts can be full, long, plain or striped. The aprons vary according to the region and can be red, white, blue, checked or in horizontal stripes. An embroidered pocket hangs from a belt. The hats are simple, usually a neat bonnet, the unmarried girls allowing their hair to show. Red or white stockings are worn with a firm black shoe.

The men wear bright yellow or black breeches tied below the knee with braid. A red, brown or striped sleeveless waistcoat is buttoned up to the neck. The long sleeved shirt is white and the stockings white, blue or black. The black shoes usually have silver buckles. The most popular head gear is the round skull cap, top hat or a peaked cap. On special occasions a frockcoat is worn.

The bright colours favoured by the Swedes reflect the importance attached to the short summer months after the long, dark winters. Red represents the flowers, blue the sky, yellow the sun and green the grass.

Traditional Dances and Style

The oldest of the Swedish dances is the circle or chain formation which is danced around the bonfires, Midsummer Maypoles, the Christmas Trees and at weddings, Sweden's links with Poland introduced to the country many dances and steps which had a strong Polish background. The most popular dance was the Polska, the name meaning Polish in English. This dance was developed by the dancing masters and now has many different forms and variations. The Hambo Polska derives from both Poland and Germany, Hambo being a corruption of Hamburg. Also from Poland came the Mazurka, first introduced into the ballrooms and later adapted by the peasants. The Waltz and the Polska likewise became incorporated into many of the couple dances. The Polka is often confused with the word Polska, but they are very different dances both in steps and rhythm. As in other parts of Europe, the English Country dances had a strong influence and many quadrilles and longways sets became adapted using basic Swedish steps and melodies. Apart from the Polish influence, the Swedes travelled and worked in Denmark, Norway, Finland and Germany and introduced many of their dances to these countries. They also brought back to Sweden new dances which they learnt. Throughout Scandinavia there was a common exchange of dances but performed with varying styles, steps and figures. There are many dances for men only in which they display their strength and agility by turning somersaults and cartwheels.

The Swedish steps are executed with precision and a strong *ballon* or lift which is developed from the action of the knee and thigh.

Customs

In common with all Scandinavian and northern countries, the spring and summer is eagerly awaited. Large Spring and Easter bonfires are made to welcome the return of the sun. At Easter when already the daylight hours are lengthening and the snow is melting, birch twigs are placed in a sunny window to sprout, the growth depicting the birth of the new season. The Easter bonfires are used to protect the land from the Nordic spirits, fire being a powerful deterrent. For good luck in the coming year people would jump over the embers.

Eggs are painted at Easter, with egg-rolling and hunting games being played. On Easter morning, breakfast always begins with eggs and whoever eats an egg sitting between a brother and sister will have their wish come true. Midsummer Eve is a holiday and a large maypole is decorated with garlands and ribbons. As the hours of darkness are limited at this time of the year, celebrations continue through the night. Small miniature maypoles are made by the children and decorated with coloured paper and flowers. A Midsummer custom is for girls to pick seven wild flowers and place them under their pillows when at night they will dream of their future husband, or meet him next day.

One of the most popular of Swedish traditions is Santa Lucia or St. Lucy's Day on December 13th. The eldest daughter of a family is chosen as the "Queen of Light"; dressed in white and with a crown of lighted candles, she offers coffee and special saffron buns (*lussekatter*) to everyone in the house.

Christmas is celebrated early when on the first Sunday in December an Advent Candle is lit and placed in the window, another candle being added each following Sunday. Christmas trees have decorations made from straw and the traditional Christmas gnome (*tomte*) and goat are given pride of place. In common with other Scandinavian countries porridge or rice pudding is eaten on Christmas Eve. If an unwedded member of the family should find the almond which has been hidden in the dish, then they will be the first to be married in the New Year, or a married person will have good luck the year through.

THE NETHERLANDS

The Dutch are a hard working people, seemingly austere; but a very friendly nation with a great sense of humour. They dance in a somewhat restrained manner without much elevation.

General Background

The Netherlands, or Holland as we call it, is a flat low-lying country made up of 11 provinces and bordered by Germany and Belgium in the east and south, and the North Sea in the west. Most English speaking people refer to the country as Holland, but to the Dutch, Holland means the two provinces of North and South Holland. The original name for Holland was Holtland, meaning a hollow or waterlogged land. Through the centuries the Dutch have, with great effort and determination, drained, cultivated and developed the land. This has been done by the skilfull construction of dykes and drainage systems, resulting in much of the *polder* or reclaimed farm lands being well below sea level. When the Roman Legions arrived in Friesland (a northern province inhabited by one of the earliest races), they found long, broad mounds which acted as primitive forms of dykes. Today 10 per cent of the land has been reclaimed and over half lies below sea level.

The persistence and hard working approach found in the character of the Dutch people gave rise to the saying "God created the world, but the Dutch made Holland". The land is a network of rivers and canals, there are almost 4,000 miles of navigable waterways, and although these have proved to be invaluable in linking regions, it has also created divisions.

The great rivers, the Rhine, Maas, Waal, Lek and Ijssel, divide the country from north to south, east to west, which has resulted in a separation between provinces and even villages. Each region has developed its own dialect, costume, customs and a strong division between Protestant and Catholics.

The North Sea provides one of the major industries — fishing, as well as linking the country with England, Scotland, Scandinavia and further afield Rotterdam has one of the largest man-made harbours in the world. It was during the period of the famous Dutch West Indian Trading Companies that Nieuw Amsterdam later to be called New York, USA, was founded and developed. Apart from fishing, the main industries are butter, cheese, milk and the cultivation of wheat, flax, pulse and madder (one of the major exports), as well as the growing of tulip bulbs (developed from a flower imported from Turkey), and Delft China.

In more recent years the Dutch have manufactured electrical equipment and cars and have developed many other industries. Throughout the country there are numerous windmills, these being used to maintain the drainage or for the grinding of corn.

Music

The simple and well accented rhythm of the folk-music of this country is usually produced today by the accordian. However, knowledge of the traditional and older types of instruments is necessary in order to understand and appreciate what has influenced its style and quality.

A type of violin has always been used in Western Europe and in olden days in Holland, it was called a *vedal*. On this kind of instrument it is usual for only a single note to be played, so the harmonic content is negligible. Therefore when the music is produced today it has a simple and unsophisticated effect.

Two other instruments of importance are the bag-pipe with its drone-like sound, and the dulcimer with its more delicate quality.

The dulcimer — flat and triangular in shape and placed on a table to be played — has a certain similarity with the cymbalom (described under Hungary); but with a very different quality of sound. The strings on the dulcimer being plucked with a plectrum; whereas the notes from the cymbalom are produced by a hammer on the strings, thus giving a much harsher quality.

Basically therefore, the music of the Netherlands is simple in harmony and rhythm.

Costume

The most popular and widely illustrated costume is that from Volendam, but this is only one of numerous costumes to be found throughout the country. Each region has developed its own style according to its occupation, religion and affluence. One of the main features is the women's bonnet. This developed from a simple cap secured with pins, which was popular in the late 16th Century, to the many and varied and elaborate bonnets now worn. Incorporated into the bonnets are gold and silver casques, beautifully worked ear-irons, lace, ribbons and embroidery. From the bonnet it is possible to tell the religion, marital status and village of the wearer.

Skirts are usually long and full which allowed plenty of room for work on the land, in the ports, or on the barges. Heavy material was used and several petticoats worn underneath which acted as protection in the winter months against the cold. In Northern Holland, Friesland and Groningen, regions of more affluent farmers and merchants, dresses were made from rich damask and imported silks. Aprons are worn in most regions, usually plain, striped or checked, exchanged for silk ones on Sundays.

Another feature of the Dutch costume are clogs. This type of footwear was both hardwearing, warm and essential to those working in the fishing and farming communities. Clogs can be painted, polished, decorated or white-washed according to the region. On Sundays or Festive occasions these are exchanged for a black buckled shoe.

In North-Holland, a farmer returning home would find a pair of black clogs by the back door. Known as "back way shoes" he would change his dirty pair for the wooden house shoes.

Fishermen favoured the full, baggy type of trousers which gave them more freedom for work on board, the farmers wearing trousers which were less full. Jackets, shirts, peaked or flat caps, varied according to the regions. Black was the most usual colour being relieved sometimes by a bright waistcoat, gold buttons or coloured scarf.

Traditional Dances and Style

Many of the dances show the influences of neighbouring countries but with slight variations. In the northern provinces, farm workers crossed from Germany to work on the prosperous Dutch farms, bringing with them the lively Polka and Waltz couples dances. Certain clapping dances, mazurka steps, gallops etc., reflect the sea-faring connections and nearness of Denmark and Sweden, many dances having counterparts in these countries. During the 16th and 17th Centuries the Scottish Brigade was one of several foreign regiments in the service of the Netherlands and many dances and music stem from this period. The trade connections made by the wealthy Friesian merchants to the British Isles and North Europe resulted in an exchange of dances and the introduction of the English Country dances and sets. Zeeland, in the south-west, had close links with Scotland through the woollen trade and one of the most popular dances of the region is the Zeeuwse Schots.

There are many popular dances known throughout the country, whilst others belong to a particular area. The action of windmills and of work are incorporated into some dances. There are several old ritual dances such as the men's Seven Jumps, found in many parts of Europe. The Egg Dance, was a solo in which the dancer performs over and around eggs placed on the ground; it is also found in Switzerland, Germany, France, Spain, Denmark and the north of England. The Pipe Dance was not unlike the Scottish Swords, but danced over crossed clay pipes as in our own Morris tradition. It was the British soldiers in the 17th Century who, during their leisure hours, introduced the making of clay pipes to the Dutch. Further afield, the Dutch took their dances to South Africa and during the Great Trek of 1835, the Voortrekkers kept alive their songs and dances as their last remaining link with Europe.

Clogs were really a working shoe, and in the evening and for dances these would be replaced by ordinary footwear. Demonstration groups frequently perform in clogs which gives a weight to the movement but at social gatherings the dance movement becomes much more boisterous.

Customs

There has always been a very strong division between Catholics and Protestants, the north and east being mainly Protestant, and the south, particularly, North Brabant and Limburg, Catholic. The many customs found in the Netherlands are generally common to both religions.

New Year is welcomed at the stroke of midnight by fireworks and ringing of bells. On this day a special gingerbread is made which is decorated with gold leaves. "Gilding" parties are held by the young girls and women to gild the cakes. Very popular at this time are large currant doughnuts called Oliebollen which are covered with sugar and look like large snowballs.

On Palm Sunday, Easter sticks or boughs called Palmpsens are decorated with flowers, eggs, bells, ribbons, sweets and biscuits. On top a replica of a hen, cock or dove used to be placed. At Easter, children hunt for hard-boiled painted eggs, and when discovered, play a game called Eiestikken in which they roll the eggs to see whose will be broken first. A special biscuit or cake is made which symbolises the sun and the life-giving rays and warmth.

Bonfires are popular in the east and south to welcome spring. As far as the smoke and light travelled so would the field have a good crop. A large sun wheel used to be placed on top of the flames and when the fire had died down people would jump over the embers. In some areas soot from the ashes would be thrown over the girls or their faces daubed if they were caught.

During Whitsun and on St. John's Day large decorated hoops would be carried through the villages in certain of the provinces.

At one time a young man would present to his fiancée a pair of clogs that he had carved and decorated; she in turn would give him a long clay pipe which would hang in their future home. Clogs placed with the heels towards the bed would ensure a peaceful night but toes pointing would mean nightmares.

December 5th, The Feast of St. Nicholas, is when the Dutch give gifts, rather than at Christmas. St. Nicholas arrives at night and children leave a clog by the fireplace full of carrots, hay and sugar for his horse. Next morning they are rewarded by finding the clog filled with sweets and oranges.

The cheese market at Alkmaar is held every Friday and has continued (apart from the war years) from 1571. The porters dressed in white with straw hats carry a type of sleigh on which the cheese is placed. When it has been weighed and auctioned it is then loaded onto the waiting barges. There is a similar market held every Thursday at Gouda.

FINLAND

The people of this northern country have rather a reserved and natural dignity which is reflected in their dancing and way of life.

General Background

Finland or Suomi, to give it its local name, is a country of vast forests and numerous lakes. Its northern territory is in the Arctic Circle and inhabited by the Lapps. The southern region is the most fertile, and where the capital Helsinki is situated. The western coastline is on the Gulf of Bothnia which separates it from Sweden; but in the north-west, it is actually joined to this country.

The Finns migrated to this area in about 100 A.D. They originated from a tribe from the east who trekked across Europe, half settling in Hungary, the rest travelling north. They belong therefore to the Finno-Ugrian language group, very different from the Teutonic which is the root of the languages spoken by other Scandinavian nations. Their original language was kept alive by peasants in the isolated country districts; but those employed or dominated by the ruling power (Sweden from the 12th Century) had to speak their language. After 800 years, they gained their independence in 1917 and now their own language flourishes.

Also invading their country at different times in their troublesome history the Russians attacked them from their eastern border; but their aggression is now over and Finland joined the United Nations in 1955.

Fishing and forestry are its main industries.

Music

The music of Finland is very interesting with beautiful melodies, often in a minor key and most likely reflecting the qualities found in Asiatic and East European styles. It is much more subtle than that of their Swedish neighbours and may of course have had inspiration from the Russians.

The Kantele is the traditional instrument. It is made of wood, triangular in shape and played in a horizontal position, the strings being plucked. In olden days there were only five strings, but now that it is coming back into favour with folk-dance groups today, we find a more complicated instrument with many more strings. The clarinet and violin too are very popular.

The music generally has simple rhythms 2/4 and 3/4 and often 5/4; but arresting harmony. This music is made familiar to the rest of the world through the works of Sibelius and Palmgren and much of their music mirrors the sound and feeling of water.

Costume

The Swedish influence is shown very strongly in the costumes, the country having been a province of Sweden for over six hundred years. The women's costumes are simple in design, and are brighter in colour in the west with vertical stripes predominating. In the east they are more sombre and the design plain. Skirts are handwoven, calf length and fairly heavy, each village having its own particular striped pattern. The long sleeved white blouses and aprons (frequently striped) are made of home-spun linen. Sleeveless bodices are striped or plain and fastened with buttons or laced up. Neat little bonnets are edged with lace, unmarried women and girls wearing a plain or embroidered headband. Silver brooches and necklaces are very popular. Blue, green, red, yellow and white are the most usual colours. The men's costume also shows strong similarities with those of Sweden, with dark knee breeches, striped waistcoats, plain or striped jackets. Silver buttons decorate the waistcoats, jackets and breeches. Sometimes a belt is ornamented with a silver design and has a knife or *puukko* suspended from it. Shoes for both men and women are strong and firm, often with a silver buckle.

Traditional Dances and Style

Like many other countries, the most ancient dance form was the chain and circle, and in olden times in Finland only performed by women.

After the 12th Century when the foreign invaders came we find the couple dance introduced. The Swedes particularly with the Polska (see under Sweden) and later the Russians with cossack steps and various forms of mime based on religious themes. The visiting English sailors brought the groups (consisting of couples) famous for their complicated ground designs. The merchants from France brought their minuet and quadrille, now performed in a rather different style.

Today their most popular dance is the Purpuri, it has many figures and changes in tempo.

A country wedding is an occasion when many kinds of dances can be seen, special ones for the bridesmaids, different ones for the guests, the dancing continuing until day-light breaks.

Particularly interesting are the dances based on the movements of birds and animals. On the coast where seals are so numerous, unusual arm positions and jumps are seen reflecting their shapes and actions (seals are believed to have been descended from Pharaoh's soldiers drowned in the Red Sea!). Forest workers observing bears, swallows and hares; farm workers with their reaping actions; domestic workers with their spinning and cooking have themes incorporated into their traditional dances.

Customs

As in other northern states, the seasons, especially the long winters and short summers, give sound reasons for festivities.

In January, on 12th night, they take their Christmas decorations down, and the day after *nuutinpaiva* is particularly for children who perform charades or entertainments and are given a special kind of sweet as a reward.

In February Kalevala Day is celebrated. This is in memory of the famous poem by Elias Lonnrot (published in 1835) which recounts the ancient legends and folk-lore of the Finns. It is now a national holiday with skiing and sleigh rides when they make special wishes for good crops.

Easter — we find the custom of painted eggs being given — also the idea of dressing up as witches and playing tricks on your neighbours. On the last day of April when St. Waldorg is honoured a strange feat is still performed today, that is of climbing up the statue on the rock in the middle of the lake in Helsinki and placing a cap on its head!

Midsummer's day is a very special celebration. The houses are decorated with birch branches; special dances performed by the lakes; a sauna taken in the evening. Finally a big bonfire known as the *Kokko* lit at mid-night (when of course it is still daylight!). The bonfires are believed to drive away evil spirits and plagues.

Maypoles are beautifully decorated with flowers and ribbons.

Christmas day is celebrated in much the same way as other countries, with the decorated tree and giving of gifts by Santa Claus but here assisted by a child dressed as an elf. In the afternoon lighted candles are placed on the graves in the local graveyard.

DENMARK

The Danish people in temperament are very out-going, friendly and relaxed in their manners and dances although their technique has similarities with Swedish and German styles. The Danes' approach to life is very different from their neighbours the Swedes and Norwegians.

General Background

Denmark is the smallest and southern-most of the Scandinavian countries, being an area about half the size of Scotland. Copenhagen, the capital city is situated in the east and was originally not only the capital of present-day Denmark, but also of Norway, Sweden, parts of Germany, countries bordering the Baltic and even parts of England. King Canute, famous for trying to stop the incoming tide, was both King of Denmark and King of England. He was also partly responsible for the building of Canterbury Cathedral. There are many English words, names of villages and towns which are of Danish-Viking origin. Those Danes who had married English wives were at one time permitted to live outside London's city walls in a settlement called Aldwych, their church being St. Clement Danes, which still exists.

Gradually, over the centuries, the Danish empire became reduced and after the First World War it consisted of one peninsula and about 500 islands. Denmark still remains an imperial power, owning the small Faeroe Islands and Greenland, the world's largest island, a territory even larger than Australia.

Denmark is not rich in natural resources, there are few minerals and no mountains to supply hydro-electric power. In the latter part of the 19th Century the Danes worked hard to make their land more productive. Consequently, it is now a country which has both an industrial and agricultural economy. Apart from butter, cheese, cream and bacon, the Danes are well known for the elegant Georg Jensen silverware and the blue and grey Royal Copenhagen porcelain. They also have an international reputation for their designs in furniture, fabrics, jewellery, kitchenware and not forgetting the famous Carlsberg and Tuborg beers.

Music

The people today in Denmark show a tremendous resurgence of interest in their traditional folk-music, particularly in the teaching of the violin.

Basically, the music is similar to that of their neighbours in the Netherlands; but with a more undulating and gentle type of melody, possibly reflecting the character of their countryside.

The harmony produced by the strings and clarinet is simple and typical of the friendly attitude of the people.

Costume

Until the beginning of the 19th Century, Denmark consisted of many small isolated villages, separated by large areas of uncultivated land. Villagers did not travel and each community developed their own individual style of dress. There are numerous different costumes to be found. Garments were mostly made from wool, woven and dyed at home. Skirts, bodices and aprons showed a variety of styles and patterns. Skirts were long and heavy, plain or striped, and worn with matching or contrasting colour, and frequently edged and decorated with woven braid or ribbon. It was thought improper to show any throat or shoulders and one or several light scarves would be held in place by pins. Aprons were always worn, whatever the occasion, and these could be checked, striped, embroidered or pleated. There are many different forms of headgear, usually a type of bonnet or scarf. A piece of linen was sometimes tied round the head, the bonnet put on top and a scarf tied round it to hold it in place. White, red, blue and green are the most popular colours.

The men wear yellow and black knee-breeches made from either wool or leather, white shorts made from flax and some form of jacket or waistcoat, either striped or plain. Buttons, usually silver, decorated the breeches, waistcoats and jackets. White knitted stockings were held in place by a garter, and a coloured scarf or bow was knotted at the neck. A brown or red knitted stocking cap with a tassel on the end was very popular, this being replaced by a black top hat for an important event. Wooden clogs used to be worn by both men and women, but on special occasions black shoes with silver buckles were worn.

Traditional Dances and Style

The chain or ring dances were the most popular and ancient forms found in Denmark. Based on the Farandole, they were danced around the Midsummer Maypoles or on long winter evenings when people gathered together in the farmhouse to celebrate a festive occasion. As communications became easier, dances from other countries spread to Scandinavia and couple dances became popular. The Minuet, Waltz and Polka passed through the ballrooms and became adapted and changed to the peasant style. Many of the dances found in Denmark have similar counterparts in other Teutonic countries but performed with slight variations in style and pattern. Dances such as Polsk, Polonaise, Varsovienne, Anglais, Francaise, Hamburger, Holstein Waltz and Rhinlander all show in their names the country of origin.

Square dances for 2 or 4 couples became very popular, these being based on the chorus and figure type of formation. A *tur* or figure dance could contain any amount of different patterns: stars or mills, baskets, circles, etc., the dancers deciding how many they wished to perform. Dancing was not always approved of by the Church, therefore many of the old dances were forgotten. Those performed today are mainly from the middle of the eighteenth to the middle of the nineteenth centuries. A dance which was found in Germany, Britain, Holland, France and Spain was the Egg Dance. Eggs were laid out in a pattern on the floor, first the man, then the woman, finally both of them dancing over and around them. At one time this was used to train the dancers in the Royal Danish Ballet to develop quick and exact footwork.

Customs

Due to climate and religious outlook, Scandinavian festivities and customs are much more personal and domestic than those found in Mediterranean countries. The many fiestas, saints' days and processions of Catholic countries have no counterpart in the northern and Lutheran practising nations. One of the main festivals in Denmark is Christmas when all the family become involved, decorating the tree, making gingerbread men, putting out a sheaf of corn for the birds and on Christmas Eve, a bowl of porridge for the *nisse*, the mysterious and ancient gnome-like creature. An important part of the decorations are the interwoven paper hearts made in red and white, the colours of the Danish flag. Very popular with children are the tall calendar candles which are marked off in 24 sections. Each day from December 1st onwards a section of the candle is lit.

Children are often given by a grandmother or aunt, an embroidered tapestry wall calendar onto which are fixed 24 hooks. A little parcel containing a gift of a sweet, chocolate or charm is hung for each day. The traditional Christmas Eve dinner always begins with rice pudding which contains one solitary almond, whoever finds the almond is given a special gift.

On the Monday before Shrove Tuesday, children awaken their parents by waving decorated birch branches. Later in the day they will put on fancy dress and go singing from door to door begging for sweet-money.

Every tenth birthday has a special celebration and is called a "Round" birthday. The 60th birthday is very important and all the family and relatives arrive for the occasion.

In common with other Scandinavian countries, Midsummer's Day, June 24th, is celebrated by lighting bonfires on the hills and along the coastline. A special Viking Festival is held each year in July at Frederikssund, North Zealand, during which old customs and ceremonies are re-enacted.

Storks have always been very popular in Denmark and Hans Christian Andersen called his country "the land of the storks". Today they are not so numerous and it is considered very lucky if a stork builds a nest on your house.

Special days are the Queen's official Birthday; May 4th marks the end of the occupation in the Second World War (and is celebrated by placing a lighted candle in the window); July 4th, American Independence Day, Denmark being one of the very few countries outside the U.S.A. to celebrate this event.

SPAIN

Spanish dancing has a strong, rhythmical interpretation with an earthy and dramatic quality.

General Background

Spain is a land of contrasts: in scenery, climate, language, music, costumes and dances. Known as the Iberian Peninsula, the north is rugged and mountainous, with its coastline on the Atlantic Ocean and the Bay of Biscay. In the south and south-east, the region favoured by thousands of holidaymakers, is the warm sun and calm Mediterranean. In the west is Portugal, and in the north-east the high mountain range of the Pyrenees acts as a border between Spain and France (there are only ten routes to pass from one country to the other). The shape of the country has been compared with a "bulls hide", the bull playing an important part in their folk lore.

The people of the Basque Region are thought to be the original inhabitants of Spain who, through a succession of invasions, were gradually driven northwards and who eventually settled in the Western Pyrenees and the coast of Biscay. They have their own language, dances, music and traditions. At the eastern end of the Pyrenees is Catalonia, a powerful region known for its independence and spirit (at one time their dance was banned as being too nationalistic). In the north-west is Galicia, the people of this region being descendents of the Celts who retreated to this corner of Spain following different colonisations. The magnificent cathedral of St. James (Santiago de Compostela) the fourth largest in Europe, rivalled Rome and Jerusalem in popularity with Pilgrims and each year thousands travelled through Europe on "The Spanish Way" to Galicia.

In the south is Andalucia, the area which was favoured by the Moors during their many centuries of rule. Although they conquered the whole of Spain and tried to capture France, it was in the south and the warmer climate that they eventually settled, before being finally evicted from Granada in 1492. In the centre is Castile, with its vast infertile plain of La Mancha (the name derived from the Arabic-*"manxu"* meaning dry and arid), famous for its windmills and the legendary Don Quixote (on which the Petipa ballet is based and the American musical "The Man of La Mancha"). It was from this region that the traditional name for the Spanish Language was derived "Castellano".

The Sixteenth Century was the Golden Age of Spain when Cortes discovered Mexico; Pizarro — Peru, and the Spanish Empire extended to the whole of Central and South America (except Brazil), Naples, Southern Italy and the Low Countries (which included the Netherlands). During this period, Catholicism also spread and the music and dances of Spain had a strong influence on the culture of other colonies. The Spaniards are a proud race; it was this pride which urged Don Quixote on his travels; the discoverers to withstand the hardships in South America, and the matador to face the bull. They have a strong religious background, Andalucia being known as "the land of Holy Mary", the emphasis being on feminine ideals rather than the strength and domination of the male.

Music

The music of Spain is very stimulating and often with a dramatic quality. It has a general appeal, whether the listeners are interested in dance or not!

The guitar is the instrument most likely to be heard in this country; it can be of various sizes and shapes and originated in the east and came to Spain via the Arabs.

The influence of Spanish music is world-wide; but particularly so in many countries of South America and Mexico. Composers of other nations have been influenced by its style and have created works for the concert hall and theatre.

It can be divided into three main types: (1) Regional or peasant style, (2) Flamenco and gipsy, (3) Theatre or concert.

The style accompanying the peasant dances of the different regions of Spain is the chief concern in this short book. Great variety too can be found in the fifteen provinces (which include the Canary Islands). In the north, chiefly Galicia and Asturias (the route of the Crusaders in olden days), a definite Celtic influence is noticed in the harmony of the music. Bag-pipes too are common to many countries, and the one used with such effect in Galicia is called the *gaitas*.

St. James (in Spanish Santiago) is the patron saint of this country; and shells play an important part in their life — decorating grottos, beating them together (instead of hand-clapping or using castanets) and in Santander they blow on a conch-shell which gives a strange and distinctive sound to their music.

In Catalonia, the north-eastern region, the music is different again, a pipe and drum provide the accompaniment to the dance, and it is interesting to note that one man plays both instruments. The small drum is attached to his left elbow, the stick in his right hand, and the fingering on the stops of the pipe is done with the left hand, a truly ambidextrous performance!

The guitar is naturally heard in the north as well as the local instruments; but the further south one goes the more predominant it becomes. The local guitars have different names in the different regions: they can also vary in tone and even in the number of strings used. In the south — Andalucia, the

26

guitar is heard at its best; and the unity between the player and dancers is fascinating to observe.

Unlike the violin which is bowed, the guitar is plucked which gives it a very definite rhythmic beat — and this again is emphasised by the dancer using hand-claps, finger-snapping, castanets etc. This rhythmic pattern can at times be quite complicated in its uneven phrasing and use of cross-accents.

Singing naturally is important in all folk dance, but in Spain it has a particular quality — a rather harsh or sometimes wailing sound. Much of the music is divided into *coplas* and *estribillos* (what we would call verse and chorus) and the dancers (and onlookers) would sing the coplas while standing still or moving with a simple walking step — while they get their breath, then burst into bouncey and more energetic movements on the estribillo.

The Flamenco style is very different and difficult for other nations to produce in its true form. It has a strong Arabic, Hebrew and Gipsy influence in its rhythm and harmony. The singing in its two categories of Cante Jondo and Cante Chico need a special study and understanding.

The theatre and concert style has been evolved from the Flamenco but without its intense and strong eastern flavour. The rhythms of bolero, jota, Sevillanas etc., have been adopted for theatre and opera presentation; but maintaining the true traditional flavour.

It is difficult to obtain music in the basic peasant style; but good gramophone recordings are available. The best place to get the music is from Union Musical Espanola, Carera de San Jeronimo 2b, Madrid.

Costumes

Apart from the USSR, Spain has probably the greatest number of dances and costumes to be found anywhere in Europe. Each province has its own costumes, and frequently those of one province bear no resemblance to those of their neighbours. The simplicity and austerity of the costumes from the mountain areas of the north contrast vividly with the richness and brilliant colouring of the south. Everywhere skirts are full and gathered which gives freedom to dance movement. In the north they are red or black and are worn with white blouses and crossover shawls. Travelling southwards and with changes of climate, skirts become floral, decorated with braid, spotted (favoured by the gipsies) or as in Valencia, made from rich damask. In this region the costumes reflect the colours associated with the Mediterranean and the orange and lemon groves as well as a strong Moslem influence in design.

Shawls are worn in most regions, in Catalonia they are made of lace, in Aragon large and fringed, in Estremadura in the west they are more like a short cape. In the north where the weather can be wet and cold, a firm shoe is worn. The rope soled, flat *alpargatas* which are laced up round the ankle are more popular in Aragon and parts of the south. A very firm and special heeled shoe is worn for all the dances which contain foot beats. Head-dresses vary from simple white handkerchiefs tied in various styles, to net *snoods*, or hats (or just a flower may be worn).

Many mens' costumes are basically knee breeches, either fastened at the knee or worn loosely over white under trousers or *pololos*. Jackets, both with or without sleeves are found in many regions as is the wide sash.

The man's costume has a certain severity and a dramatic style, colours are often dark and this tends to highlight the woman's dress and stress the contrast of the Spanish character. Hats vary from the flat crowned, straight brimmed Cordobes hats found in Andalucia which give good protection from the sun, to the red berets of the Basques, the moslem influenced turban type worn in Aragon, and the stocking cap in Catalonia. *Alpargatas* or shoes are worn according to the region and for gipsy dances a small ankle boot with a strong heel.

Traditional Dances and Style

The dances of Spain, like the country, are very varied and range from the balletic and elevated movements of the Basques (where the step, Pas de Basque originated), to the gipsies of Andalucia with foot beats, hand claps, castanets, or the dance performed by the choir boys twice a year in Seville Cathedral. No country has such a diversity of styles.

Spanish dancing can be divided into four main categories — Flamenco or gipsy, Classical Spanish, Peasant or Regional and the Theatre Style. The most popular is Flamenco, a highly stylised and technical dance style which requires a special study. The gipsies originated in India and through a succession of migrations eventually settled in Andalucia where they developed their own very distinctive music and dance. The gipsies have a very strong sense of rhythm and many of their dances are performed to a vocal and guitar accompaniment, the dancer, singer and musician blending skilfully together. Classical Spanish was the style which became popular in the Nineteenth Century and which blended ballet technique with Spanish port de bras and carriage. Essentially a theatre dance, one of its famous exponents was Fanny Elssler, known for her interpretation of the Cachucha.

The theatre or stylised form, were choreographed dance arrangements which adapted the Flamenco movements to suit both dancers and audiences, who found the true Flamenco dance too profound for the theatre.

Throughout Spain there is a wealth of regional or folk dances mainly for couples or pairs in longways sets or circles. There are several dances for one man and two girls or as in Asturias, one man courts six or eight girls! One of the most popular of the couple dances is the Jota which has many variations, steps and styles according to the region. The most vigorous form is found in Aragon in the north-east and the most elegant is from Valencia. The Fandango is another couple dance which, like the Jota, has many different interpretations. Many of the regional dances are in the verse (*copla*) and chorus (*estribillo*) arrangement, frequently with a repeating chorus between verses. There are many dances which have Greek, Roman and particularly Arab backgrounds in their formation, themes, steps and music. The Sardana (the once banned national dance from Catalonia) reflects the old Greek circle dance or even an earlier sun worshipping ritual. There are many stick dances, found mainly in the north and are similar to the English Morris.

Castanets are used and played either attached to the middle finger in the peasant style or on the thumb. When these are not used the dancers snap their fingers, or sometimes use a tambourine. All Spanish dances have a strong rhythmical interpretation which is expressed in foot beats (*taconeo*) of the Flamenco style, or in the use of the castanets, finger-snapping, or hand-clapping in counter rhythm. Little or no physical contact is made with one's partner but there is always present a strong, passionate awareness and communication.

Customs

All over Spain there are Romerias, Verbenas, Ferias, Fallas, all called Fiestas. Every village and town has its own celebration, many with strong religious backgrounds. Holy Week is known throughout the country and the beautifully carved statues are taken from the churches and carried through the streets accompanied by religious songs (*saeta*) and the sound of trumpets. For hardworking people, the Fiesta breaks the monotony of everyday life and is an occasion for wearing traditional costumes, and for music and dancing.

In the north a typical festival can include trials of strength and skill such as weight-lifting (the Basques lift great blocks of stone), tree-felling, hay-cutting, ball games, regattas, boat races and throwing the caber. In Leon, wrestling matches are popular and in the Canary Islands the wrestlers, called "cockerels" are named after the sport of cock-fighting which was once so popular. All these events are predominantly for men, as is the famous bull fiesta at Pamplona in Navarre, which celebrates the Patron Saint, St. Fermin. This is a display of courage as young bulls are let loose in the crowded streets.

Romerias are village pilgrimages to the shrine of the local Patron Saint and are always an occasion for singing and dancing. The altar is decorated with flowers, candles and small offerings. The pilgrims will travel many miles in covered carts and sometimes may be escorted by the horsemen from the Andalucian plain.

Verbenas are not rural, but town fiestas, and are usually held at night and are in honour of a saint. Madrid celebrates a series from spring to autumn, one of the most popular being St. Anthony de la Florida. On this day dressmakers dip their pins into the font and ask for a husband, St. Anthony being the match-making Saint.

As in most parts of Europe, St. Joseph's Day is celebrated with bonfires. The idea was thought to have originated from the Guild of Carpenters who burnt their wooden shavings on this day, St. Joseph being their Patron Saint. Huge papier-mache *fallas* or giants are eventually burned on the fires, all except the one judged the best, the *Ninot*. In some regions a large cardboard bull "the fire bull" is lit and pushed through the streets until it finally burns out.

In the south there are many fiestas which commemorate the conquest of the Moors by the Christians, with mock battles, gunpowder and fireworks.

On Christmas Eve in some mountain areas of the north, a fire is left in the grate all night. This is in case the Virgin Mary passes by with her newly born child, she can warm herself and dry the nappies! Sometimes the best chair is left for her to sit on and on Christmas morning the children look anxiously to see if it has been used.

PORTUGAL

The Portuguese have a somewhat fatalistic approach to life, and their dances vary from rather slow movements to the quick and bouncy running styles.

General Background

Portugal, part of the Iberian Peninsula, is bordered on the East by Spain and its long coastline on the west by the mighty Atlantic Ocean; therefore fishing is a very important industry. It has always been a great seafaring nation and one of England's oldest allies, particularly since Charles II married Catharine of Braganza. It has had a turbulent history, chiefly with Spain; but evidence of its once great naval power and conquests is finding the Portuguese language spoken today in Brazil and the Azores.

Because of its shape (long from North to South, narrow East to West), extreme variations in climate are found in its five provinces. In the mountainous North (Minho) it is very cold in the winter; nevertheless an important wine-growing area — the grapes from there being used for their famous port. In the centre it is more agricultural, corn and rye being grown, also where the famous cork forests exist. In the South, the popular Algarve, it is a much warmer climate, and again an important wine and orange growing area.

An easy-going nation, hospitable and courteous.

Music

Because the Moors and Arabs occupied most of Iberia in ancient times, the music today retains this eastern influence in much of its harmony and certainly in the quality of the singing voice. The Portuguese however, when singing a Fado do not have quite such a harsh quality as the Spaniard singing Flamenco, the sound being quite different from that of the folk-singers of northern and western Europe.

The guitar is the most usual instrument heard in this country; it is larger and more mellow in tone than the kind found in Spain. Drums are very popular; they are small, often square-shaped and hung from a cord round the player's neck. Fingers, rather than drum-sticks are used to produce interesting rhythms. Tambourines too are used for percussion. Bag-pipes (like the gaita from northern Spain) are found in the North, and flutes are used in combination with all these instruments.

The Fado (meaning fate) is a musical form found in all districts; it is usually improvised and is of a plaintive and soulful quality: nearly always in 4/4 time and with cross-accents or syncopation which gives it an added interest. Most time-signatures are simple, but a little casual in phrasing.

Costume

The exuberant spirit and independence of the Portuguese people is expressed in the bright and colourful costumes, even the fishermen wear clothes that are far from sombre.

The women's skirts throughout Portugal are fairly full, allowing plenty of movement, for work on the seashore, in the fields, vineyards or for dancing. It is not uncommon to tuck the back hem of the skirt into the belt and so form a type of divided skirt or trouser. The most colourful costume comes from the Minho region in the North, the heavy striped skirt is woven at home, each village having a different design. The bodice is embroidered with wool and a heart-shaped pocket is hung from the waist (similar to those found in Scandinavia). Bright cotton skirts with a broad sash tied round the hips are worn by the women of lower Minho, whilst those from the fishing village of Nazaré wear tartan skirts and aprons. In the southern Algarve coloured skirts are worn with attractive high-necked, puffed sleeved blouses. Due to the heat of the sun, shade is given by a square coloured scarve folded into a triangle and worn loosely over the head shading the back of the neck. A black felt hat is then placed on top which acts as a protection for carrying goods on the head. In some regions a round pad known as a "mother-in law" replaces the hat.

In Coastal areas shoes are rarely worn, except on special occasions. In the North a backless mule is popular which restricts the feet being lifted too high when dancing. In the South, neat little boots are worn and dances containing beats are always executed with a firm shoe.

The men's costumes are not as colourful as the women's, apart from tartan shirts which are popular in many regions particularly in Nazare where the fishermen also favour tartan trousers. It was thought that these designs were copied from the Scottish regiments who in the early 19th Century fought in the Peninsular wars. The black trousers and jackets which are found in many regions complement the women's colourful costumes and show the more serious aspect of the Portuguese character. The *campinos* of the bull breeding area of the Ribatejo spend a great deal of time on horse-back, where breeches are favoured with red sashes and waistcoats. Apart from the fishermen, black leather shoes are most usual; black felt hats and the popular stocking cap.

Traditional Dances and Style

Dance movements are obviously influenced by the shape of the costume and the *Vira* is a good example of this (*Vira* means to turn). It is found in every district, and varies in rhythm and pattern; but always with predominately turning steps. The idea is to show off the full skirts worn by the girls and these can be gathered, flared or pleated. The dance consists of couples within groups either in a square — circle — or longways set. It can vary in time signature; for example the *Vira* from Nazaré is in 2/4 time and that from Lisbon is in 3/4.

Fandangos are much simpler in technique than those found in Spain. They are often performed in barns on wooden threshing floors so that the dancers can emphasise the beats made by their strong shoes to the firm 3/4 rhythm. (Flat rope-soled shoes or even bare feet are usually only found in the coastal area.)

The *Corridinho* (meaning to run) is a quick and exciting dance found in the South.

The exact pattern of our strip-the-willow is found in a dance in the Lisbon area, obviously taught by our soldiers in the Peninsula War. Interesting stick-dances done by men are possibly derived from or have a similarity to our Morris dances.

When castanets are used they are played in a very simple manner with single beats. The castanet is attached to the middle finger of each hand by a cord from which hangs several coloured ribbons. Finger snapping is very popular and accompanies nearly every dance.

Customs

The Portuguese are mostly Roman Catholic; and all folk-lore is based on religion — originally pagan, now of course Christian.

There are roughly twenty-three saints' days observed during the year, too many to list here. Therefore, it might suffice to note some of the local customs that are interesting and which pertain to many of the festivals or *romerias* (a *romeria* takes place in a country area, a festival or fiesta in a town).

Jumping over the embers of a bonfire is practised in many European countries; but in Portugal a young man and girl join hands and do this together — then he offers her a purple thistle, which has been scorched in the flames. She plants this and if it flourishes, then their love prospers.

Candles too are found everywhere, and are symbolic — their flames thought to carry our prayers to heaven (Sicilians claim to have invented them!). The Portuguese have a charming way of carrying them to the church; either holding the base tucked into a lace-edged handkerchief or decorating the base with flowers and ribbons — the idea being to protect one from any hot wax which might melt and burn one's hands.

Festivals celebrated at night can be very picturesque with lights coming from wrought-iron lanterns, paper lantersn (made in the shapes of castles, or ships), pine-cones soaked in oil, hollowed pumkins and onions which are scattered in the grass and hillsides like hundreds of glowworms.

In January too, a farmer on the day of San Vicente, will carry a lighted resin torch to a hilltop — if the wind blows it out — it signifies a good harvest.

The devil was always associated with swine, so on the way to a *romeria* a peasant would hang a ham, a piece of bacon or a sausage on a tree in order to protect his family from evil.

Flowers, both real and artificial, ribbons and paper streamers are used for special head-dresses — and for outlining jars (called *cantarhinhas*) carried on the girls' heads.

The carts are beautifully painted and the oxen have garlands of flowers and ribbons round their horns and necks, thus making a very colourful procession to the church.

Birds, particularly green parrots, flowers, cockerels, fish and hearts are incorporated into the beautifully embroidered designs seen in some of the costumes and table-cloths.

The bride still wears the lovely gold-filigree pendant ear-rings made in the shape of a rose or heart.

At Pentecost bunches of poppies, yellow daisies, and wheat are bought from merchants standing near the church. These are symbolic of health — wealth and good living.

ITALY

The Italians are a romantic and flirtatious people and their dancing reflects these qualities. The dances are either quick and vivacious, or slow and sentimental.

General Background

Italy, which is shaped like a boot, has two long coastlines, the Mediterranean on the west with the islands of Sardinia, Elba and Capri, and the Adriatic on the east, with Sicily at the toe. In the north the country shares borders with France, Switzerland, Austria and Yugoslavia.

The beauty of the country, its geographical position and its climate, together with its important trade routes, made Italy vulnerable to attack. The powerful Roman Empire lasted over 400 years and its culture extended throughout Europe (including Britain) and Asia. When it collapsed, Italy became the target for many invasions. At one time the north-east belonged to Austria and briefly, France occupied the north-west.

The powerful Bourbons and Spain ruled the south and Sicily. In the 14th and 15th Centuries large regions became dominated by influential families: the Sforzas, the d'Estes, the Medicis as well as individual cities such as Venice, Florence, Genoa, Pisa, Rome and the Papal States. All of these were centres of commerce as well as culture. The many divisions created intrigues and rivalry, but apart from the internal wars it was a great period of art which has never been surpassed. Each city, region and ruling family vied with each other in presenting the best in painting, sculpture and architecture. It was only in 1870 that Italy finally became a united country with Rome as its Capital.

Italy is fairly rich in vegetation although limited by mountain ranges, the Alps in the north, the Appenine mountains which stretched throughout the country diagonally from the north-west to the south-east. Wine and olive oil are the main products; Italy with France, rating as the largest wine-producing countries in Europe and the largest in the world for olive oil.

Situated in the north are many car, mechanical and electrical industries. It is a land of contrasts and this is shown by the people who enjoy life: they are romantic and flirtatious and their dancing reflects these qualities. The dances are either quick, noisy and expressive or at other times they can be leisurely and taking things as they come.

Music

Singing to accompany the dance is common to every country and the Italians are famous for their good voices, particularly the appealing quality of the tenors.

Their sense of harmony is not particularly inspiring, harmonizing in thirds is very typical and this has rather a sentimental effect.

An interesting feature is the strange onomatopoeic sounds sometimes made by folk-singers; these are interspersed between the actual words of the song, and are supposed to imitate (or simulate) the sound of ancient instruments such as a primitive kind of pipe called *sulittu* or *launed-das* and no longer in use. Some kind of wood-wind, or guitar is still the most usual and efficient if accompanying the tarantella, as its lively 6/8 rhythm must have a staccato quality necessary to produce the light and brisk movement of the dancers.

Instruments today of course vary in different districts: flutes, bag-pipes, and a monotonous kind of drum beat are heard everywhere.

The accordian, relatively new, roughly 150 years old, is very popular and played most enthusiastically.

Costume

The many divisions of the country led to a wealth of different costumes, customs and music. There are now eighteen regions in Italy, each with its own style of dress. In the north the costumes reflect Austrian, French or Swiss influences, especially in the head-dresses. In the south with its warmer climate the people are different in character and the costumes change considerably. Many of the costumes, embroidery and designs show a strong resemblance to those of the Renaissance period which so influenced western Europe as well as Italy.

Women's skirts are wide, gathered and often pleated in various ways. Apart from Naples the skirts are usually long and made of wool, damask, heavy taffeta etc. Blouses are of white linen or cotton with many different styles of sleeve, as well as neckline. Bodices also vary, being laced at the front or back and cut high or low. Usually dark in colour, they are very firm and act as a corset.

Aprons can be most elaborate and decorative. The head-dresses in the central and southern regions are the *tovaglia*. The material is folded in many ways with a piece down the back to protect the neck from the sun. Shoes range from low-heeled black leather to the soft and laced up *ciocie*.

Colours change according to the locality with blues, greens and purples mainly in the north. Bright reds, green and maroon in the south with blue predominating in the areas by the sea.

Men's costume is less elaborate: breeches or long trousers are worn with a wide striped or brightly coloured sash. Long sleeved shirts of white linen, a colourful waistcoat or jacket trimmed with gold buttons. A dark felt hat in various styles is found in many regions, whilst the knitted stocking cap is worn by the fishermen, red in Naples and black or dark blue in Sicily. White, coloured or striped stockings are worn with black shoes on which there are silver buckles; alternatively there is the heel-less leather *ciocie*.

Traditional Dances and Style

The Italians have always been known for their music and dance. It was Catherine de Medici, who in 1581, presented to the French Court "Le Ballet Comique de la Reine", and this was to influence dance throughout Europe.

In 1820 Carlo Blasis, the famous dancing master from Milan, set down a system of dance upon which the present system of classical ballet technique is based.

In common with most Latin countries, couple dances predominate: the dancers (unlike those of northern Europe) having very little physical contact and the ballroom or peasant holds very rarely used. Religious upbringing was strict and although dancing was permitted, close holds were not encouraged; a daughter would be very closely watched by her mother or chaperone.

The dances are lively and energetic, the climate allowing the festivities to take place outdoors. Dances such as the *Saltarello* (from Saltare, meaning to jump) are mentioned in Greek and Roman times. There are numerous variations and names for this dance and it is popular in many parts of Italy.

Other dances show the influence of the various courts and the Spanish occupation of the south. Quadrilles, square sets and pattern dances reflect the interchange between the peasants and the court. Many of the dances have a flirtatious approach, reflecting the Italian's romantic nature. There are dances which use a mirror, a candlestick or a chair. Others show the action of washing.

One of the most popular and well-known of the southern dances is the Tarantella. Thought to have come from the town of Taranto it is also associated with the spider Tarantula. It has many variations ranging from the simple to the highly stylised. Movements from this dance are depicted on Greek vases and on the walls at Pompeii. Often improvised it can be accompanied by castanets or tambourines and the steps are small and lively. In some regions the dances have a smooth lilting style which reflects another aspect of this romantic race.

Customs

In common with Portugal and Spain, Italy has a wealth of Saints Days, pilgrimages, processions and carnivals. It is a country strong in its Catholic faith with the Vatican at the centre. The various *feste* bring colour, devotion and excitement to poor and hard working communities and a *festa* is a great occasion in which everyone takes part.

In many processions the Saints and Holy Figures are carried through the streets and sometimes taken out to sea.

In Palermo at Easter there are mock battles between the devils and the angels, when the two statues, representing the Madonna and Christ are barred from making their way.

In many regions animals are taken to church to be blessed. A well known *festa* is the Palio at Sienna, in which a horse race takes place around the Piazza del Campo. This is preceded by colourful flag waving dancers, the participants resplendent in medieval costumes.

Corpus Christi, in early summer is associated with flowers.

At Genzano, near Rome, the streets leading to the church are carpeted with flowers in beautiful designs and religious motifs, the day preceding having been spent by everyone gathering blooms for this event.

Bournonville used this theme for his ballet "The Flower Festival at Genzano".

In Florence during the month of May there is held a "Cricket" Festival in which it is good luck if you can find and catch a cricket or *grille*. This little insect is a symbol of rebirth, Spring and good fortune. The cricket is put into a cage and if he chirps during the first three days of his captivity the owner will have good fortune for a year.

At Christmas the children make a family crib or *Presepio* and on December 23rd the shepherds, called *Zampognari*, arrive in Rome from the mountains to play and sing.

Children in other areas dress up in imitation of them. Presents are given on Twelfth Night of the Feast of Epiphany. On this day a benevolent old woman called "Befana" (a corruption of Epiphania) will arrive and fill the childrens' shoes with presents, but leaves only pieces of charcoal for the naughty ones. She carries a bell in one hand and a cane in the other.

THE U.S.S.R.

Broad and expansive movement with a flowing quality and emphasis into the ground.

General Background

Occupying one-sixth of the world's surface, the U.S.S.R. is comprised of 15 major republics, each with its own music, dances, costumes, languages and folklore. The country extends from east to west for 7,000 miles and from the bleak polar climate in the north to the subtropical south, 2,500 miles away. When a new day dawns in Vladivostock in the east, it is still evening in the west. The U.S.S.R. (Union of Soviet Socialist Republics or CCCP in the Cyrillic characters), borders on to 12 countries, has a coastline on to 13 seas, which include the Baltic, Black, Caspian and the Sea of Japan. The 15 constituent republics also include autonomous republics, regions and areas, so within the Soviet Union there are more than 100 different nations and nationalities.

The Soviet Union can roughly be divided into two sections, the European Russia (Russia, Ukraine, Byelorussia, the Baltic groups etc.) all situated in the west, which are mainly populated by the Eastern Slav group. The east, Transcaucasia and Central Asia, have strong Tartar and Mongol links.

Old Russia has had a history of wars and invasions, from the early Vikings (the name Russia is thought to be derived from RUS, a word given by the Slavs to the Viking traders and settlers), followed by the Swedes, Poles, Turks, Tartars, French and Germans. Throughout the centuries what was known as Russia gradually extended and many neighbouring countries became absorbed into its present size.

People in the west refer to the whole of the U.S.S.R. as Russia, but Russia in fact now refers to the RSFSR (Russian Soviet Federal Socialist Republic) which is the largest of the republics and contains the cities of Moscow and Leningrad. Moscow is the capital of both the Russian Republic and the Soviet Union. Leningrad was only founded in 1703 by Peter the Great (he was nearly seven feet tall), who wished to form a link with the west and create a European style capital. Known as St Petersburg, it became the home of the Czars, as well as the centre for ballet and the arts. It was Peter the Great who also gradually regained the land from the Swedes.

The Ukraine lies in the south-west and is the second largest republic in population. The land is mostly flat, very fertile and is one of the major farming areas for wheat. Very different in outlook from the Russians, the Ukrainians tend to be quicker (as reflected in their music and dances). For many years they were under Polish domination and only as a result of the Second World War did Western Ukraine become part of the Soviet Union. The Ukraine is the region of the Cossacks (from the Tartar word meaning "vagabond"), who were originally nomadic tribes who settled in the Ukraine, taking the name of the region: Don Cossacks from the River Don or the famous Zaporozhye from an early settlement on the Dnieper River. The Cossacks became known for their courage and daring deeds and were used as front line fighters. A law unto themselves, they would say "The Cossack does not doff his hat, even to the Czar". Taras Bulba, made famous in a novel by Gogol and later made into a ballet, was a Cossack chief from Zaporozhye.

In the west is Byelorussia or White Russia; a large republic covered with lakes, forests and wheat fields. Bordered by Russia in the east and the Ukraine in the south, their outlook is more in line with their neighbours in the north west rather than the Ukraine.

The three Baltic republics of Latvia, Estonia and Lithuania are situated on the north-west coast and the Baltic Sea. The people of these republics have strong links with Western Europe, Germany, Poland and Sweden and their beautiful cities and towns reflect the three very different nationalities. The University at Vilnius (Lithuania) is now the oldest in the Soviet Union. The three countries which had been independent became part of the U.S.S.R. after the Second World War.

Moldavia is one of the smallest republics and is situated in the south-west. In the west it borders on to Romania and in the north, east and south-east, the Ukraine. Part of the country was once known as Bessarabia and in 1940 became part of the Moldavian Republic. A region well known for its vines, it produces some of the finest wines and brandies in the U.S.S.R. A bunch of grapes forms part of the country's emblem.

The Transcaucasian republics of Georgia, Armenia and Azerbaijan lie between the Black Sea and the Caspian Sea, sharing borders with Turkey and Iran. It is a region which lies between Europe, the Middle East and Western Asia, where East meets West, with the strong impact of Christian and Moslem cultures. This interesting region with its high Caucasian mountain range, the highest in Europe, is full of legends. It was to these shores that the Argonauts sailed in search of the Golden Fleece and Prometheus (who stole the fire from the gods and gave it to man) was bound to a cliff in these mountains.

Central Asia is very different from the rest of the U.S.S.R. Consisting of five republics (Kazakhstan, Kirghizia, Tajikstan, Turkmenia and Uzbekistan) it is a region of mountains, deserts, cotton plantations, orchards and vineyards. The old Silk Route caravans passed through this area on their way to the Far East. It is a land of mosques, domes and minarets and is associated with such legendary figures as Alexander the Great, Genghis Khan and Tamerlaine (buried at Samarkand-Uzbekistan).

To the north and east lies Siberia, an area of over 4 million square miles containing vast stretches of forests, lakes and rivers. The famous Trans-Siberian Railway covers over 6,000 miles and takes 8 days from Moscow to the east coast. Inaugurated in 1891 it is the longest continuous railway in the world.

Music

Russian music is as varied as the people and their languages of the many regions that constitute what is now called the U.S.S.R. However, first to consider the European section and particularly the part around Moscow, one finds that the music nearly always has a melodic line that is within the range of the voice: and singing is the operative word. Russia has always produced good singers and their choirs are world famous: they, like the Welsh, have the ability to harmonise in a spontaneous and interesting manner. If, then, one listens to music with four or five parts in the harmony, it produces a very rich and dramatic quality. (This effect is reproduced on the piano with full rich chords, a very different construction from the music played for English or French dances.)

The majority of the peasant dances are in a 2/4 or 4/4 rhythm and nearly always in long phrases (very different from the Czech form). Because of the choral associations the music gives a flowing quality to the steps of the dancers, and an expansive dimension to the movement.

The balalika is one of the most popular instruments, but its chief value is keeping the tempo under control, which may vary considerably in one dance. An interesting point is that the variations in speed tend to occur gradually in their music which is very different from the sudden changes in tempi found in the Hungarian style.

The composers who have based their work on folk themes are numerous, but familiar to most people are the names of Tschaikovsky, Rachmaninov, Glazunov, Borodin, Pachulski, Gliere, Liadov and Mussorgski. By this last composer it is interesting to know that his "Night on a bare mountain" is based on the festivities associated with St John's Eve — a mid-summer event celebrated in every European country.

In the Transcaucasian region the music still has a flowing quality (particularly in Georgia) but the harmony has a much more eastern bias due to their proximity with other countries and their use of the pentatonic scale. On the eastern side of the Caspian Sea, the music is even more Asiatic in its content, the influence of China being very evident.

In these republics all use stringed instruments which are based on a violin but with different sizes, shapes and number of strings. Again variations of a lute are found everywhere.

Percussion too is produced in unusual ways, the multiplicity of sounds is most intriguing. In Uzbekistan they hit two stones together, or beat a large tambourine called a *daf*. In the Caucasus the beat is produced by a kind of wooden rattle.

Piano music is rather difficult to obtain from this part of the U.S.S.R.; but quite a good selection of gramophone records is available.

Some composers who have been influenced by the unusual music of these regions are Ippolitov-Ivanov, Rimsky-Korsakov, Khachaturian, Terepchine.

Costumes

In a country as large as the U.S.S.R. there are thousands of costumes which have many differences according to regions. In the Russian Republic one of the most popular costumes is the women's Sarafan, a type of pinafore dress which is worn over a white sleeved blouse with embroidered full or three-quarter length sleeves. The sarafan can be plain in colour, or be of a floral or brocade design and decorated with braid and buttons. The type of sarafan varies, some are long and heavy and worn with a loose jacket as in the north, others are short and calf length. The crown type of headdress or *Kokoshnik* also varies and is worn with the hair in a long plait (unmarried girls). The length, fullness and weight of the skirt gives the dance movement a flowing quality. A firm character shoe is worn.

The men's costume in this region is less varied and is a style found in many other republics with slight differences. A loose Russian shirt worn outside the trousers, and tied round the waist with a cord, has a stand-up collar and a side opening. The hem of the shirt, the cuffs and the neck opening are sometimes embroidered. Dark trousers are tucked into black boots. The trousers in the R.S.F.S.R. are tighter than those of the Ukraine.

In the Ukraine, the most typical costume for women is the white, long-sleeved shift which is embroidered in the hem and sleeves. Over the shift is worn a tight-fitting, short skirt which is open at the front from waist to hem, which allows the dancer plenty of movement. The skirt is in a square design and is short enough to show the embroidered hem of the shift below. For festive occasions a sleeveless jacket is worn, together with a flowered head-dress and long ribbons. A white or coloured apron covers the opening in the skirt. Red boots are usually worn.

The men wear full, baggy trousers tucked into red boots. The fullness of the trousers allow the men to perform the strong, athletic steps of this region.

A white shirt with a centre opening is worn inside the trousers and a broad sash tied round the waist.

The Moldavian costume is different again. Full, short skirts, sometimes pleated, with an apron at front and back. Close fitting bodices or fur edged waistcoats are worn over white blouses. The men's white shirt is worn over black or white trousers which are tucked into black boots. A waistcoat similar to the girls' and an astrakhan fur hat.

The fullness of the skirts in the Byelorussia costumes reflects both their Polish and Russian background as do the men's striped trousers. The costumes of the Baltic republics each have their own distinctive style and show their strong individuality.

In the Transcaucasus, the long, full skirts limit the steps to a gliding walk, the emphasis being placed on the carriage of the upper body and the use of the arms. The veiled headdress shows the strong Moslem links. The men wear tight trousers, soft black boots and three-quarter length, tight fitting coats. Simple and economic in design, the costumes reflect the spartan pattern of living and highlight the beauty and elegance of the women.

In Central Asia the costumes are numerous, many being based on the kaftan style of tunic-dress worn with long trousers. The wearing of trousers by women enabled them to sit cross-legged on the floor (chairs not being used) and also allowed kneeling actions in the dances which in a skirt would be difficult and ugly. Little round hats, worn over their plaited hair are very popular. Crossing from the west into the east, neat, low-heeled shoes, sometimes with a slight turned up toe, replace the boots and firmer shoes in the west. The men also wear the loose Asiatic type of coat, over trousers, but those of the nomadic and horse riding background wear a boot. Hats vary from turbans to the shaggy goat or sheep skin hats in Turkmenia.

Traditional Dance and Style

Each region of the U.S.S.R. has its own specific dance styles and characteristics but a feature of the dances from the European Russian Republics is their feeling of movement and space. The flat, agricultural land and the vast distances are reflected in the way the dancers cover the ground. The oldest form of dance is the circle or *Khorovod* which in its original form was frequently sung, the dancers expressing the words with various actions such as sowing millet or flax. Many of the *Khorovods* celebrated spring, summer, the harvest or the weather, as in the Ukrainian-Metelitza or the Russian-Pourga-Viyouga which create the illusion of a snowstorm. There were also *Khorovods* for girls only, for couples and in which a couple or an individual would dance in the centre. Many of the dances and particularly the "solos" in the centre were improvised and took the form of a light-hearted competition, the boys showing off their strength and the girls their lyrical qualities. In the dances of western U.S.S.R. and especially in those of the Asian Republics, the men predominate with strong, athletic steps which highlight the graceful movements of the girls.

In time the sung dances were accompanied by instruments and new dance forms were introduced with the quadrille and lancers formations. These dances were popular in the ballrooms of the 19th Century and were taken and adapted by the peasants who introduced their own particular regional steps and styles. In the dances of the Russian Republic (R.S.F.S.R.) beats, stamps and claps are a feature as in such dances as *Pereplias* (an urban or town dance rather than country).

The dances of the Ukraine also have an improvised approach but the style is much quicker and lighter than that of Russian and do not contain beats and stamps. The men perform very spectacular steps which were developed from the Cossacks and which eventually became part of the Ukrainian background. Cossack dance movement is strictly for men. There are no girl's dances in this style. The dances of Byelorussia are a blend of both the Russian and Ukrainian styles, the movement covering the ground well. Very different are the dances from Moldavia which show the influence of Romania, the dances being based on runs, hops, skips and with an easy swing in the body; there are no solos or difficult and strenuous jumps for the men, the steps being the same for both men and women. The dances from the Baltic region although very individual, show their links with Scandinavia, Germany and Poland.

The people of the Transcaucasian Republics dance in a completely different way, their language, the musical sound, the writing are in complete contrast to those in western U.S.S.R. Like so many mountain people, they are strong, proud and independent. Within the mountains there are numerous groups who have developed quite separately from each other. The Georgians, as in the other Republics, show very different styles for men and women. The feature of the women's dances being the gliding walks and beautiful arm movements. The men are fierce, excellent fighters and horsemen, quick and sharp, they move swiftly and noiselessly in their soft, tight boots, in which they often dance on the knuckles of their toes. Dancing space is limited in mountain areas and often dangerous, the men will walk in front of the women testing the ground for safety. The villages or *Aouls* are situated amongst the high peaks, not unlike eagles' nests, a bird they much admired and which the men copied in their movements, and the women in their flowing actions. The women are tall and considered to be the most beautiful in the U.S.S.R. The dances of Central Asia feature the use of the women's arms and hands rather than on complicated steps. The steps are small and the movements delicate which suit the Asiatic physique. Many of the dances are improvised and based on various work themes. The men dance in complete contrast, at one time many of the people were nomadic and strong actions of horse-riding are found in their dances.

Customs

The people of the U.S.S.R. have always been interested in legends, folk stories, myths and heroic deeds which would be recalled during the dark winters. One of the most popular characters is the old witch Baba Yaga, but there are also various household spirits who were thought to live in or behind the stove or in the barn. A bowl of food was left out over night for if they were not respected they would play tricks on the family or the cattle. When a family moved house the fire irons were always taken, if not the spirit could be upset and burn the house down.

The birch tree and its branches are very much esteemed in the U.S.S.R. as a symbol of light. In the western regions, the branches were used to make torches and carried round the fields to protect the crops. The origin of the birch was thought to be Scandinavian as it was associated with the God Thor and symbolised the return of spring and of light after the winter. When a boy was born it was a custom to plant a birch tree, the stronger the tree grew, so would the child flourish.

At weddings grain and hops would be thrown over the newly married couple to symbolise a healthy and prosperous marriage. The bride would also throw some money or bread down the well or into the river to ensure she would have a fruitful marriage. On the wedding cake or loaf it was a tradition to have two doves representing fertility, wealth and happiness. After the wedding the bride would have to cover her head and her long plaits cut off.

Spring and the summer months are always anxiously awaited and the season officially begins when the first larks are seen in March. Little cakes used to be made in the shape of birds and sold everywhere. Another sign that spring was coming was when the ice began to crack on the lakes and rivers, the first sound heralded better weather and young girls and women began to unpack their lighter clothes once more.

To bake on Friday was considered unlucky and if by any chance it was Good Friday then the woman's hands would turn to wood.

Easter has always been of special importance in the U.S.S.R. and the decorated and painted eggs are amongst the finest in Europe, each republic having their own designs and methods of colouring them. Eggs would be exchanged, games played with eggs, and even an egg would be buried beneath the house to mark the end of winter and the beginning of spring.

People would also visit the cemetery and hang eggs on the graves not wanting anyone to be left out of the Easter celebration. Some of the most beautiful eggs were made by the court jeweller Fabergé, as gifts for the Czar and his family.

In Estonia special cakes are made from the first sheaf of corn cut, and in Lithuania a loaf is made which contains all the different types of grain, one for each member of the family. In the Baltic republics, Christmas trees are decorated with ornaments made of straw.

In most parts of western Russia and in countries with a Slavonic background bread and salt are offered to guests as an act of friendship. A handkerchief plays an important part, not only to cover the head but in several dances and when the lady offered it to a man it represented either a favour, courtship, or the invitation to participate in the next dance.

In the Ukraine on St John's day or Midsummer's Eve, the girls make wreaths and throw them into the river. Should they float or sink will foretell whether they will be married or not, a custom also found in Poland and other countries.

In the Transcaucasian Republics and especially in Georgia, men's daggers were highly prized and these would be passed down from father to son. Many of them would have a message or proverb engraved on the blade such as "I am slow to offend, but quick to avenge". When the new moon appeared it was good luck to make the sign of the cross with the dagger towards the sky. If two men began a fight they would cease immediately if a lady dropped her headdress between them.

In the Asian republics, tea (unlike bread and salt of the west) is always offered to guests. Asian girls are much admired for their long plaits and in Uzbekistan a girl will arrange her hair into as many plaits as possible, the more she has the more she is favoured.

BULGARIA

A style of dance which shows similarities with other Balkan States, but much more complicated in rhythm.

General Background

Bulgaria is the most eastern of the Balkan states — It is a very interesting country, spectacular scenery of plains and mountains, and with extremes of climate — very cold winters, and hot, dry summers.

It has a relatively short coastline on its eastern border — the Black Sea — not a great expanse of water, but an important link with the U.S.S.R.

Moving in a clockwise direction round the country, in the south-east corner it borders on to Turkey: due south it has a frontier with Greece — on the western side Yugoslavia and in the north it is separated from Romania by the famous river, the Danube.

The country itself is divided into six states — Shopski in the west where the capital Sophia is situated; Mizia; Thrace; Dobruja; Rodopi; and Privin. The Greeks, Thracians, Jugoslavs and Macedonians, all Byzantines, left their influence on the culture of the Bulgarians. The Turks, however, occupied their country for more than five hundred years and obviously had the greatest effect and were a very dominating and aggressive race.

The capital Sophia is a very beautiful city dominated by a spectacular cathedral with its golden dome, a relatively recent building erected in memory of Alexander Nevsky, a Russian who helped them drive out the invading Turks in 1878. The work on the cathedral was started in 1904 and took eight years to complete.

Agriculture is the basic occupation of the people: their exports of cereals, vegetables, all kinds of fruit; tobacco; sunflower oil; wine etc., provide the main source of income for their country.

Since becoming a communist state in 1944, industries are becoming more important but as there are relatively few cities in the country, farming is still of primary importance.

Music

Thrace, the southern part of Bulgaria has the delightful legend that the Greek God Orpheus visited this region and with his famous lute created melodies which exist to this day in some of their folk tunes.

The Bulgarians are a most musical race, nearly every family has someone who plays a musical instrument and all seem to be able to sing and harmonise together in a most creative and natural manner.

The main instruments used are the *gaida* a form of bagpipe; the *kavel* and the *droyenka*, types of flute; the *gadoulka* or rebec and tamboura, stringed instruments. Like other countries in eastern Europe, the importance of the use of drums is considerable.

The harmony of the music shows a strong influence from the east, particularly from the Turks; but for people in the west the most difficult aspect of their music is the rhythm.

Quite a number of the popular dances are in simple time signatures; but the following are quite common i.e. 5/8, 7/8, 9/8, 11/16, 13/16.

5/8 means five quavers in a bar, and in their well-known dance *Paidushko* meaning limping, the division is 3, then 2 counts.

7/8 like the Kalamatinos in neighbouring Greece, the seven quavers are subdivided 3, 2, 2.

9/8 The 9 quavers here not divided as we would expect into 3 sets of 3 like our compound triple-time, but into 4 pulses of 2, 2, 2, 3.

11/16 or 11/8 This rhythm has 5 pulses in the bar and can be written as 5 quavers, one of them being dotted; or if 11/16 when these will be two semi-quavers to each of 4 pulses and 3 semi-quavers to the fifth pulse. This elongated pulse or beat may occur on the first beat of the bar, the middle or the last.

13/16 is divided in the same principle as 11/16 but with six main pulses one having the elongated or extra half value, for example—the 13 semi-quavers are divided thus, 2, 2, 2, 2, 2, 3. This may appear complicated but in actual fact the stressed or elongated beat usually occurs when a stronger movement is demanded (either with elevation or depth) and once the step-sequence is set and mastered by the dancer, the difficulty is minimised.

Among the modern composers of Bulgaria who base their compositions on folk-themes are Krsimir Kyurkchiyski, Lyubomir Pipkov, Georgi Kostov, Pancho Vladizherov, Vassil Kazakdjiev, Mrin Goleminov. The better known Bela Bartok, the famous Hungarian, wrote an interesting suite of piano pieces based on Bulgarian folk-tunes.

Costume

In common with other Balkan countries, the women's costume is based on the long sleeved, white smock over which is worn various types of skirts, aprons, jackets and coats.

In the north a gathered or finely pleated knee length over-skirt or apron is worn. This fastens at the waist with an opening down the front. A second apron is then worn to cover the gap. The over-skirt is woven in perpendicular stripes, the smaller apron being in horizontal patterns, red, black and orange being popular colours. Knitted socks in various colours are worn with the flat Balkan leather sandal. In central and southern regions a blue, black or red sleeveless tunic or overdress (*sukman*) is found. Also popular is a type of overdress made like a coat with a front opening over which is worn a large apron to cover the gap. White, patterned or striped stockings, with the flat leather *opanki* are found in most regions. Belts are very popular everywhere, these can be woven or of leather with elaborate silver buckles. Married women cover their hair but young girls wear simple headscarves unless it is a festive occasion when flowers and coins decorate the special headdresses. The handwoven smocks and overdresses are heavy and often restricted in the amount of material used, this caused the dance steps to be small, the accent being on rhythm rather than on elevation and large movements.

There are two main styles of men's costumes; one consists of tight white trousers decorated with black cord and worn with a white shirt, a sleeveless white or black jacket, or a knee length white coat, white socks and the traditional leather sandals. The other costume is based on full, baggy trousers usually tucked into thick white socks or having long strips of woollen or flaxen material wound round the lower leg.

Various types of jacket and broad waistbands complete the costume. Many of the dances have a belt hold, the men's belts being without any ornamented buckles. Everywhere the black sheepskin hat is found.

The freedom of the trousers allows the men to dance with more speed, stronger movements, lifted knees and deep knee bends.

Traditional dances and style

The Bulgarians are very proud of their heritage of traditional dance and today it is kept to a very high standard. It is performed frequently in the country festivals. In the towns there are many opportunities for everyone to learn them from experts; in clubs, universities, schools and in the recreational classes for workers in factories. (It is interesting to note that most of the dance teachers are men: no private schools exist; everything is run by the State.)

The number of dance groups supported by the government is most significant; over 2,500 of an amateur status, and at least 20 professionals who often perform overseas.

The style of their dance naturally varies according to the terrain and region and the influence of the adjoining country. Basically, all the Balkan States have rather a relaxed type of movement, particularly in the foot-work. The steps are usually small and kept under the body; this probably due to the fact that the duration of a dance is so lengthy that longer steps would be too exhausting. As far as the women are concerned their heavy skirts restrict movement. The emphasis on the beat is into the ground; but not heavy — the men making more stress than the women. The Bulgarians maintain that this action shows their contempt and resistance to the Turkish invader. They have a saying about a heavy dancer: "He stamps like a horse and shakes like a bear".

The form of the dance is usually a circle, chain or line and is known as a *horo*. The dancers can be linked together by joined hands in the "W" position, holding the belt of the next dancer; with hands on each other's shoulders; or the basket hold. Each village has its own special *horo*, and they may vary in speed from slow, to very fast. The chain is usually led by a man who is easily identified by the red or white handkerchief which he carries in his right hand, and uses it like a conductor with his baton, in order to direct any change of step or pattern.

The trembling or shaking movement is found chiefly in Shopski, the western state adjacent to Yugoslavia, but stronger in style than theirs. Again the strong emphasis is to show their defiance of the Turk, as well as to show off the jewellery worn by the women. In some dances men wear cattle bells attached to their belts, and coins on their costumes which add a jingly sound to their movements.

Couple dances are unusual; but the Rachenitza is an important excep-tion. Each region has its own style; but it is always in 7/16 time. It usually starts off as a solo with interesting improvisation of steps, the soloist is then joined by a girl and the dance continues as a duet. This dance is seen at most festive occasions, especially weddings, when everyone joins in to form a circle or chain.

Like other countries — dances based on work themes are numerous, and mimetic actions based on bread-making, digging, wood-chopping and the potter turning the lathe etc.

The movements of birds, particularly the eagle, of animals such as the fox, hare, horse and bear give an added interest and meaning to many dances.

In some of the dances for men only, they are seen wearing animal masks which are associated with fertility rites. These dances are very spectacular and boisterous; the performers carry wooden swords with which they tap the spectators on their shoulders in order to bring them good luck.

There is a saying that "The Bulgarians walk slowly but dance quickly".

Customs

As noted in other countries the customs practised by peasants originated from pagan times — then kept alive by associating them with celebrations in connection with incidents in the life of Christ; or in honour of special saints. This interest too is shown as subjects or themes for ballets, plays and musical compositions. Quite apart from the pleasure of the peasants having a reason for a holiday and a party, it affords an opportunity and an excuse for them to practice traditional customs and superstitions which can be very colourful and amusing.

The baking of bread or cakes into different shapes is very popular: the dough being moulded into various designs according to the occasion being celebrated — birds, animals, bunches of grapes or ears of corn etc.

The use of blue beads to ward off the evil eye is an interesting legacy of the Turkish occupation; these may be used for necklaces or fixed on to collars worn by animals.

Different seasons have their special customs and beginning with New Year's Day: the children may carry a stick or branch called a *survaknitza*. This branch is decorated with coloured wools or popcorn threaded on a string. The children wander round the village tapping on the doors of the houses in order to bring the occupants good luck. If they are lucky, the housewife gives them a kind of biscuit or bread roll baked in the form of a little circle which is then hooked over the *survaknitza*.

Fortune telling for young girls is practiced at this time too. They drop flowers attached to a ring into a large copper bowl of water; when these are then withdrawn their destiny is foretold.

In the next month, February, the pruning of the vines occurs, and on the 14th, St. Trifon's Day is celebrated by much singing and dancing. Wreathes and sickles are carried in procession and are symbolic of the work they do.

On March 1st, a very popular token of good-luck is the gift of the *Martenitza*. This gift consists of red and white tassels which symbolise health and happiness (today this may be given at any time of the year). If received on March 1st, it is specially significant because the recipient must keep it till the first swallow or stork is seen in the spring, then bury it under a stone, thus ensuring one's wishes will be fulfilled!

April, when Easter occurs, painted eggs, being symbolic of resurrection, are found in many countries, but in Bulgaria they have an interesting method of presenting them, that is tucked into a round ceremonial loaf in a decorative design. Spring is also welcomed by the young girls wearing lovely head-dresses made of fresh flowers.

May is specially the month when the shepherds take a major part in the celebrations and decorated crooks are carried by the dancers.

On May 24th two brothers, St. Cyril and St. Methodius are honoured as great writers and founders of the Cyrillic alphabet.

Many customs still exist to protect the crops from evil spirits; one seen in Thrace is when young girls walk round the fields carrying a very small child in elaborate costume and known as St. Enjo's bride.

Herbs too are important in protecting from evil, illness or ghosts. They are wrapped in a handkerchief and always carried especially on a journey.

Dances to do with fires in mid-summer occur in other countries; but on June 2nd and 3rd St. Constantine and St. Elena's day, the Bulgarians dance on the hot embers of the fire.

Weddings are always festive occasions and a *horo* is danced round the *Oruglica*, a flag or banner decorated with flowers and ribbons. The *Rachenitsa* too is performed and gives an opportunity for individuals to show off.

In western Europe pitchers, or buckets are often attached to a yoke and are the usual methods of carrying water. In Bulgaria an unusual way of supporting the yoke or *kobilitsa* is not across the back, but on one shoulder the containers being one in front of the body and the other behind. Instead of buckets two large copper bowls are used; this gives rise to another amusing custom: if a young man is attracted to the girl carrying the *kobilitsa*, he will take a drink from a bowl; if she doesn't want to encourage him, she walks on — if interested she plucks a flower from her head-dress and gives it to him.

GREECE

A style of dance which has much in common with other Balkan states but with a certain elegance and interesting rhythms.

General Background

Greece, a country roughly the size of England, but of great contrasts in its landscape — mountains and plains, arable land as well as much that is infertile.

It is the south-eastern region of the Balkans and the link between Europe, Asia and Africa.

In the north it is bounded by **Albania, Yugoslavia and Bulgaria** and separated from them by a massive mountain range: in the north-eastern corner the Euros river separates it from Turkey. This land frontier extends for roughly 500 miles. The coastline is much more extensive, 9,375 miles, and is bounded on the western side by the Ionian Sea, on the eastern side the Aegean Sea, and on the south by the Sea of Crete which is part of the Mediterranean.

Because of the contrasts in the terrain, the climate has great variations in temperature. Many of the inhabited areas of the country are over 3,000 feet above sea level, therefore colder at night and with often quite a considerable snow-fall in the winter. (There are many mountains of over 6,000 feet, and Mount Olympus — the traditional home of the gods — is 9,550 feet.) The plains and the coastal areas as well as the numerous islands surrounding the mainland have a typical Mediterranean climate. Volcanoes exist, and earth-quakes are not uncommon.

A great deal of the land is unproductive due to lack of care and probably the casual approach to life by the peasant: and because of the general erosion of the soil and also through the years it has been overgrazed by goats (over 3 million exist today).

However, where agriculture flourishes, vineyards are found, also citrus fruits, olives, wheat, tobacco and cotton.

Fishing is a natural occupation for a country with a long coast-line, and for the people of the many islands. Most of the islands are inhabited, the two largest being Crete and Cyprus.

The historic buildings: temples, theatres, stadium and monasteries, often only spectacular ruins today, are world famous: but evidence of their dramatic, colourful and classical history. Greek plays are still performed today, and the pagan rites once performed in the temples to their mythological gods are usually the background of many strange customs of present times.

Due to the turbulent history of the invaders of their land — the Greeks are a curious mixture of east and west. As a race they are usually dark-haired and good-looking. The men take a dominant place in every aspect of their lives — even in the home the women play a minor role.

Music

The Ottoman Empire has left its mark on many countries in eastern Europe, and in Greece the Turkish influence is evident in much of their music. The Turks were not evicted until 1827. The melodic line is interesting but the harmony is simple. However, the rhythm is the most intriguing—9/8, not what is expected — compound triple time; the but nine quavers divided into 2223, then 7/8 divided into 3.2.2. 5/4 either 2, 3, or 3, 2. Many dances are performed too, to the simpler times of 3/8 and 2/4; but often with uneven phrasing. The rhythm of 7/8 is called *epitritos,* and 2/4 *dactilos*; these rhythms are based on the poetic metre of the syllables of words from the ancient Greek dramas.

The music today can be divided into two distinct styles, the village and city forms: this is due to the type of instruments used. The country people favour wood-wind, and an unusual type of violin called *kritiki lyra,* with drums accenting the rhythmic beat. It is only during this century that the city musicians adopted the *bouzouki.* The distinctive sound of the *bouzouki* is always associated now with Greece especially through the films "Zorba the Greek", and "Never on Sunday".

Modern composers who have based their compositions on folk-themes are: Hadzidakis, Theodorakis and Xarhckos.

Costume

The Greek costumes are amongst the most interesting and colourful of all the Balkan countries. The women make their dresses to impress rather than to show off or flatter the body and in so doing incorporated all the various handicrafts of weaving, embroidery and metal work. There are numerous costumes to be found, all showing a great variety of different styles and designs, many reflecting the Greek and Byzantine traditions. Greece being such a land of contrasts, the costumes vary from those worn in the mountain regions, the plains and on the islands. Most of the women's costumes are based on a long under-dress or smock, frequently embroidered on the hem and sleeves. Over this is worn a type of tunic or over-dress, ranging in design and material, brocade being very popular. Coats or jackets of varying lengths, complete the costume. In some regions, especially in Crete, white baggy trousers are worn under the smock.

There are numerous different headdresses (which denote the married or single state), aprons and belts. Gold and silver chains and coins (showing a girl's dowry) are worn on the headdress, round the neck, waist or on the aprons. The women of Castellorizo (The Dodecanese) wear a great many rings and they show these off by walking about with their arms crossed over their chests. Many of the skirts are long, a particularly beautiful one is the *Amalia* named after the wife of King Otho, the first King of Greece, who came to the throne in 1837. When the skirts are short, white, black or patterned, knitted socks are then worn. Shoes vary and can be the flat *tasarouhia* with red pom-poms on the toes, a backless type mule, or a black shoe with a low heel. The proud carriage of the women, their dignity in the lovely costumes, the elaborate headdresses, give to the dance movements a very different style from those found in other Balkan countries. The flat *tasarouhia* shoe is very firm but made with a slight ridge along the sole which enables the dancers to use the foot with more pressure.

The men's costumes can be divided into two styles, those based on the baggy or long trousers and those on the white skirt or *foustanella*. When the *foustanella* is worn, a white shirt, waistcoat, broad sash and the *tasarouhia* pom-pommed shoes complete the costume. In the regions where the men wear the baggy trousers, the trousers are tucked into black boots (white in Crete), and are worn together with a variety of different styles of waistcoats and jackets. Black round caps, or hats, are made from lambswool, velvet, felt or a type of red fez with a long tassel is very popular.

Traditional dances and style

The dances of Greece can be divided into three main groups:
1. Coastal which are lilting, perhaps reflecting the movements of the sea.
2. The plains — here the movement has more emphasis into the ground.
3. The mountains — these are usually slower in tempo and with more bounce in the steps.

For centuries dance has been associated with Greece. In pre-Christian times when all the other countries in Europe lived a primitive life-style — Greece was cultured in all the arts. Evidence of this is seen today in vase paintings and sculptures depicting dancers performing ritualistic movements to the gods of ancient mythology. Terpsichore, the goddess of dance is still honoured today, and every village has a special area kept apart for this purpose and called the *chorostasi* (or *choros*).

The dance and mime performed by the chorus in Greek plays depict the character and theme of the mythological god associated with the drama. These movements are often reflected in the folk-dances of this age, and rituals still observed by priests in the Greek Orthodox Church.

Folk-dances usually take place in the open-air; but in Greece also in the tavernas — both in the villages and cities.

Everyone is invited to join in (even tourists!). The dances are usually in chain or circular formation. The steps themselves are not difficult but the rhythms can be quite intricate. There is usually great mobility in the knees and feet. In all types of dances the steps are short. The women keep the feet near to the ground, in many regions the skirts are long and a certain demureness is expected of them.

The movement of the men is much stronger in contrast, and their role more important in every aspect — a fact common to all countries in eastern Europe but particularly so in Greece.

The formation of the dances can be for men only — women only — as well as mixed groups. There are only a few couple dances.

The most famous dance today is undoubtedly the *Kalamatianos*. It is in 7/8 time in a chain formation led by a man and danced in quite a quick tempo. The leader holds a handkerchief in his right hand with which he signals to the rest of the dancers variations in the basic steps, or changes in floor patterns. Originally this dance was much slower in tempo, and rather sad in its harmonic content and historic theme (the women of Souli committing suicide by hurling themselves off the rock of Zalonga rather than submitting to the yoke or domination of the conquering Turk). The rhythmic walking action of this dance is a good example of the use of *epaulement*, and makes it an attractive spectacle for the onlooker. The *Syrtos* is another form or variation of *Kalamatianos* but in a simple 2/4 rhythm.

There are many dances in which only men take part — the most usual one being *Tsamikos*: in 3/8 time and in an uneven timing of slow (12) quick (3). Here the men show off their strength and agility competing among themselves and executing the many variations that occur in this dance. It is interesting to note that so many of these war-like movements common to the men's work are directly descended from the Pyrrhic dances of ancient Greece. (The Pyrrhic style was a form of military training — chiefly for men, but also for women fighters known as Amazons.)

Hassapikos, another popular dance, originating from Turkey, is a legacy of the 400 years of their occupation. *Pentozali*, or *Criticos* is an interesting dance originating from Crete. *Zeybeck* on the mainland, emulates the flight of an eagle.

Of the dances for women only — *E Tratta* is an interesting one where they perform movements associated with the use of fishing nets. *Yerakina*, an attractive one where they jingle their bracelets to attract the attention of a man to rescue a maiden who has fallen down a well — is among many others based on a special theme.

Of couple dances, *Ballos* is the best known — but varying in its form in different districts. It started in one of the Greek islands and is probably of

Venetian origin. It is now popular on the mainland; basically a courtship dance and in a simple 2/4 rhythm.

Arm movements imitating the wings of birds and their actions in mating habits give an interesting aspect to many dances.

The *Syrtos* is an important dance because at any gathering it is used as an introduction to entice people on to the dancing floor.

The dances of the islands all have their own local variations of style and tradition. Crete is specially interesting with their strong and bouncey movements. Particularly connected with this island is the *Farandole* (the interpretation of the well known myth of Theseus and the Minataur) variations of this dance are now found in other countries in Europe.

Customs

Of all European nations, the Greeks seem to have the strongest family ties. Once the marrying of a daughter with a dowry was essential: also at one time the oldest son would never marry until all his sisters had found husbands! Today these customs are not so arbitrary. However, still today, particularly in village life the family alliances are very strong, and moral codes strictly upheld — especially by the women. The man is in supreme command of the house and its economic activities as well as pursuits of all the members of the family. This attitude is reflected in their dances, women always taking the subordinate part.

In the Macedonian region when a girl became formally betrothed, she had to present her future in-laws with hand-knitted socks which she had made herself. Another custom is to have a lantern or candle blessed in the church, carry it home without it blowing out, which is then a sign that marriage will take place within the year. After a wedding the bride, before entering her new home, would crush a pomegranate with her foot as a sign of fertility.

In Crete if a girl is engaged or married she wears a knife in her belt.

At a wedding the guests throw sweets, coins, barley, chick-peas and rice over the bride and groom as symbols of plenty.

As a race they are very noisy, volatile, sensuous people, usually unpunctual, but always most hospitable.

When excitement gets out of control at a gathering of dancers in a taverna (probably through much drinking of *ouzo* or *retsina*) they pick up their glasses or crockery and smash them on the floor. This habit is certainly discouraged today, but it can still happen!

One of their industries is the cultivation of silk-worms, and a red silk handkerchief is a prized possession. It is often carried by the leader in a chain-dance; and/or given as a love token — an alternative to red roses in western Europe.

A festival — whether of religious or political origin — is always an excuse for a holiday — and there are so many, at least two or three every month.

Easter is the most important festival — spring being the awakening of nature in all its forms. Many fertility rites are still practised which are symbolic and expressive — such as the giving of almond blossom, red peppers, leeks, rice, and many varieties of vegetables.

Every village has its own special saint where ancient practices are still observed — such as fire-walking, wearing of goats' tails — movements imitating birds, particularly the flight of the eagle.

As in many other countries, eggs are associated with Easter. In Greece on the Sunday, they are rolled down a slope which recalls the Angel of the Lord rolling back the stone from Christ's tomb. The Thursday before Easter, known as Red Thursday, the eggs are dyed red and buried in each corner of a vineyard to protect the grapes from damage by hail.

In the autumn when the corn-sheaves had been stacked in the field, the farmer's wife would bring a pitcher of water, sprinkle the hands of the labourers and the ground round the sheath to bring good luck.

Many customs can be traced back to ancient mythology—an interesting one occurs in January during the halcyon days when the king-fisher is honoured. The goddess Hera in her anger turned Halcyone the daughter of Aeolis (god of wind) into a king-fisher. Then Artemis, goddess of the moon is venerated by the ground pattern of the semi-circle used so frequently in their chain dances. The Greek chorus of ancient time comes from the word *choros* — which in turn was the origin of the words — *horo, hora, horovad* and *kolo* — all terms used in other countries whose dances use this half-moon design. In the past when dancing these chains when men and women took part, they were always linked together with handkerchiefs: to hold a girl by the hand would signify that marriage was intended.

YUGOSLAVIA

An interesting form of folk-dance, rather relaxed in footwork, but stimulating in rhythm.

General Background

Yugoslavia is a country of violent contrasts, in scenery, climate, language and religion. It is situated geographically at the crossroads of Europe and subsequently has had a turbulent history. The country is elongated in shape and runs diagonally from north-west to south-east with a long coastline on the Adriatic Sea which separates it from Italy. Yugoslavia was a name given to this country after the First World War and meaning union of southern-slavs. The 22 million people who now hold Yugoslav citizenship consist of no fewer than six major regions all of which are subdivided into various ethnic zones. The major regions are called: Slovenia, Croatia, Bosnia-Hercegovina, Montenegro, Macedonia and Serbia. Beginning at the north-west corner the frontiers border on to Italy, Austria, Hungary; then travelling eastward — Romania, Bulgaria; to the south-east Greece, and south-west Albania.

There are many conflicting aspects of this country's character due to the many changes of government and different conquering nations. At one time much of the Adriatic Coast belonged to Italy, the north was part of Austria and the powerful Turkish nation swept through the country via the Balkan states. Like the landscape which ranges from green Alpine pastures in the north to bare brown mountain ranges in the south-west, the Yugoslav people are as varied in their languages, dialects and religions. There are three main languages, Slovene, Serbo-Croat and Macedonian, and two alphabets: Latin in the mainly Catholic north, and Cyrillic in the rest of the country. With the three main religions, Roman Catholic, Eastern Orthodox and Islam, there are many interesting cathedrals, monasteries and mosques to be found.

The main industries and occupations are as varied as the country. The great plain of northern Croatia is very fertile but much of the remainder of the country supports agriculture, vineyards, and the raising of sheep and cattle. Groups of villages now join together in co-operatives and share farming implements and marketing facilities. Many high mountain areas such as the Dalmation coast and the Slovenian Alps are completely barren. Due to the long coastline, fishing is an important trade.

Over the country as a whole local skills of textile manufacture, weaving, embroidery, pottery and wood carving are slowly dying out and designs are being debased by outside influences. Efforts are being made to conserve and revive local skills in these areas. Carpets and rug-making are found in most regions. In Bosnia-Hercegovina, Macedonia and the Albanian region of Southern Serbia beautiful gold and silver filigree work is an important feature.

Music

Of all the conquering nations, the Turks (who occupied Bosnia and Hercegovina, Serbia and Macedonia) had the greatest effect on the music of Yugoslavia. (They were finally evicted at the end of the First World War, although a large part of Serbia was independent in 1876.) Croatia and Slovenia were part of the Austro-Hungarian Empire, and much of the coastal region was part of Italy. Macedonia is today divided between Yugoslavia, Greece and Bulgaria. All the regions have their distinct traditions often derived from the kind of instruments used, and which in turn affect the manner of dancing. The different languages and stress of syllables in words have also influenced the various rhythms.

There is a great variety of instruments of all kinds, which are still in general use and retained in certain villages. There are many wind instruments — single open ended pipes, single and double mouth blown whistle pipes. Many kinds of single and double bagpipes, some without a drone. Various stringed instruments ranging from the ancient three stringed fiddle to the more modern *tamburitza* band plus the modern groups of clarinet, accordion and violin. There is a variety of drums — a large double sided type, and small "egg cup" shaped ceramic drum or the metal single skinned drums.

The harmonic and rhythmic structure of the music is often unusual (especially in Macedonia) the musical form being very different from that found in Scandinavia and Western Europe. Rhythms equivalent to 5/4, 7/8, 9/8 or 11/8, or combinations of these are quite common and with cross rhythms and cross accents and uneven phrases being typical of many of their dance tunes. The length of a dance and music and phrase are often asymetrical and not equally allied to the step sequences and this is usually termed cross phrasing. In Croatia and parts of Serbia and Slovenia, dances are often accompanied by singing. The augmented second (see glossary) is an interval of common use found in the melodic line of much of the folk music.

The rattle or jingling of the coins decorating the costumes of both men and women often provide an interesting percussive sound to the melody. In some region dances are accompanied only by the sound made by the coins — the reason being that in bygone days the Turks wouldn't allow them to play their own traditional tunes.

Costumes

There has been a gradual decline in the wearing of traditional clothes but these can still be seen on special occasions such as weddings, feast days or at folk festivals which attract the genuine village groups.

Yugoslavia's turbulent history is reflected in many of the costumes and the 500 years of Turkish domination in the Central and Southern regions influenced many of the belts, veils, trousers, jackets, hats and jewellery.

In the fertile region of Slovenia, the costumes are similar to those of Austria, under whose domination it was for many years. Skirts are full, aprons large, the hats decorative, bodices tight and the shoes low-heeled and firm, very different from the rest of Yugoslavia. The men wear breeches tucked into boots, waistcoats and brimmed hats. The people of Croatia also came under the Austrian–Hungarian rule but unlike Slovenia they retained their individuality which is shown in the diversity of costumes.

In many parts of coastal Croatia the women wear the basic long-sleeved smock with various types of aprons which are frequently covered with coins. On the Hungarian border full pleated skirts, colourful embroidered blouses, floral shawls are worn by the women, whilst the men wear white linen, full trousers and boots, the costumes reflecting those of their neighbours.

In the fertile northern plains of Croatia, full sleeved blouses, multi-pleated skirts and aprons are all richly embroidered.

In Bosnia-Hercegovina many of the costumes have beautiful designs in gold embroidery but in Montenegro, the smallest republic, the costumes are much more ornate with rich metallic work on the jackets, and imported factory made materials.

Serbia, the largest republic, has many different kinds of costumes. The most typical women's costume is based on a long smock or shift, a richly braided jacket, a long pleated woollen skirt which is sometimes divided in the front and hooked up at the back. The men have trousers cut like riding breeches, and richly braided dark jackets. Richly knitted socks are popular with both men and women. In the south the Turkish influence is very pronounced, and as in Bosnia many women wear full trousers or *shalvar*.

Macedonia has very old preserved traditions in its garments, which until recently have survived with most items intact. Many of the villages had their own individual styles and could be identified by both the cut and embroidery. Many of the women's costumes are very elaborate and are now only worn for very special occasions. The costumes are heavily embroidered and braided, aprons are heavy and chains with silver coins are worn on the aprons, hung from belts or round the neck. Because of constant wars, the women wore the family wealth in the form of silver jewellery and coins which was both portable and represented her dowry.

Costumes in most regions are heavy, the material frequently being made from hemp or wool. Skirts were also long and sometimes narrow, the width of the woven material limiting the fullness. Embroidery, braid, coins, jackets etc., all added to the weight and so restricted the dance steps and movement, placing the accent on rhythm and small steps.

Red, white, black and blue are the basic colours, with orange and yellow. The embroidery is frequently red, the red tones symbolise the blood shed in battle against the Turks, and the dark colours framing the red represents the nations' sorrow at its lost freedom. In Serbia a flower that often appears in patterns is the peony. There is a tradition that red peonies grew from the blood shed by the Serbian soldiers who died at Kosovo.

The men have much more freedom in their costume which is also reflected in their dances. The trousers can be full and baggy as in Hercegovina and parts of Croatia, or they can be tight fitting, as worn in Serbia and parts of Macedonia. A *Fustenalla* type of skirt worn over white trousers which are tucked into knee-length patterned stockings are also found in Macedonia. Head wear varies from a type of red fez to knotted turbans or black sheepskin caps.

Both men and women wear the *opanci* or leather sandals which vary from region to region. Some are heeled, some flat, some are secured by leather thongs, others by string and some by metal buckles. The Serbian variety can be very elaborately plaited and have turned up toes. The Macedonian kind are the most basic.

Traditional Dances and Style

The style of movement and the use of the upper body varies across the country. Precision of footwork is not always apparent because of the very small vibrant steps, and the trembling of the body. These movements are sometimes difficult to associate with the musical phrase and beat. In other regions the movement is lighter, and more ground covered but still with a trembling of the body. Some dances have varying movements in each direction, or have dance and music phrases which are asymetrical. In some regions the men improvise on a basic step. The dances in the eastern and southern regions can be very energetic for both men and women, but the latter in more restricted movement. Some of the men's "heroic" dances need tremendous virility and strength. The women's movements are more gentle and keep nearer to the ground due to their long skirts, religious principles and their subservience to the men. Movements generally have an emphasis into the ground which is typical of all countries in Eastern Europe. However, this does not mean that they lack elevation.

Couple dances do exist, particularly in Slovenia, and two well-known courtship dances from Serbia are the *Kutunka* and *Lilka*. However, the circle and chain dances are quite the most general and are known as the closed or open *Kolo*. The dancers can be joined together with various kinds of hand holds, or linked together by handkerchiefs, strings of beads, small towels or by gripping each other's belts or shoulders.

Sometimes these chain dances are performed without any musical accompaniment; the timing being maintained by the jingling sound of the women's jewellery and coins. This lack of music was originally intended to express their sense of independence under the Turkish regime and their dislike of their overlords who banned their own national melodies. Another reason for so much jewellery and metal ornaments being worn was that during the Turkish occupation it was always necessary to carry one's wealth on one's person!

Most *Kolos* increase the tempo during the dance until a very lively speed is attained. The leader (nearly always a man) sets the steps and changes of pattern and is usually of skilled technique and ability.

The Macedonians are considered the most able and interesting of the folk-dancers and perform two main types of Kolo, known as Oro and Horo in Macedonia. The Lesnoto meaning "easy dance" has a relaxed walking movement, and the Teskoto are quicker and more spirited in style.

Dances may be for men only — women only — or mixed.

The dances may be performed for hours on end, and this is one of the reasons why the steps are short and foot-work kept under the body.

Customs

Orthodox weddings are always an occasion for dancing, and when many interesting customs are observed. One particularly amusing one found in Macedonia is the *Svekroino* or mother-in-law's dance. The bridegroom's mother leads the dance with a sieve and some bread carried on her head! or sometime a pitcher of wine.

At a Moslem wedding seen in Montenegro: someone would carry a small mirror to catch the rays of the sun and shine it on the bride and her guests in order to protect them from the evil eye.

In Serbia ritual *Kolos* are danced round a bonfire on Easter Monday and Midsummer Night. On St. George's day and Whitsun women perform the *Kraljice*. They wear tall pointed head-dresses and carry red silk banners decorated with floral motifs. In this area too we find the *Momacko* a competitive dance for men only, where they show off their skills and agility — the women who watch award the prize to the best performer. Again only performed by men are the sword dances. (The swords nowadays usually made of wood). The swords are brandished above their heads and round their bodies.

Plums, the basis of *slivovic* (their national drink), and cherries feature in many of their customs and have a special significance in their festivals.

In Serbia a crown or wreath is made from the last sheaf of wheat harvested. On May Day the doors and windows of the houses are decorated with flowers and greenery. In some villages the young men collect flowers and make spectacular arrangements during the night on the window, or garden gate of the home of their girl-friend. Next morning every girl hopes to see a beautiful display!

In Bosnia, during the summer, the shepherds drive their sheep into the mountains for better pasturage, and to while away the time they carve decorative objects to give to their girl-friend, or for wedding presents on their return in the autumn. Distaffs, spindles, chests, pipes or wooden mugs are the most usual.

ROMANIA

A form of dance with strongly accented rhythms; "jigging" actions of the arms and a downward emphasis in the foot-work.

General Background

The rich and mountainous land of Romania is situated in the south-east of Europe surrounded by four neighbouring countries and a 153 miles coastline on to the Black Sea in the south-west. In the north and north-east the country shares a long border with the U.S.S.R., in the south with Bulgaria, the south-west with Yugoslavia and in the west, Hungary.

The country is divided into seven main regions, Moldavia, Dobrudja, Wallachia (where the capital Bucharest is situated), Oltenia, Banat, Transylvania and Maramures. In the centre is the Transylvania Plateau, and forming an arc, surrounding the Plateau and dividing north from south, are the impressive Carpathian Mountains and Transylvanian Alps. The Carpathians are like the backbone of Europe as they curve down through several countries.

Romania has many natural resources such as oil and coal, but it is also rich in agriculture. The forest regions supply a great deal of timber; the land produces many crops, with orchards and vineyards, as well as good grazing land for sheep and cattle, all of which play an important part in folklore.

The political boundaries have changed considerably during the history of the country which has been one of continual disturbance. The Hungarians (or Magyars) occupied Transylvania from the 9th Century and remained in this part of the land until the Austro-Hungarian Empire was divided up in 1918. The powerful Turkish Sultans as they swept through the Balkans into Europe met with many defeats in Romania. In Wallachia (in the south), Vlad the Impaler briefly defeated the Turks, but his appalling cruelty earned him immortality as the inspiration for the legend of Dracula. The greatest hero was Michael the Brave, not only did he make a last stand against the Turkish domination, but in 1601 he united all Romania under one rule, the first and last time until 1918.

Moldavia in the north-east, and especially Bessarabia and Bukovina in the north of this region changed frontiers with Russia several times, finally becoming part of the Soviet Union. The Orthodox Church and Roman Catholicism are the main religions and there are many fine examples of ancient monasteries and wooden churches, built from the wood from the numerous forests. In the Middle Ages so frequently did the enemy cross the borders that the peasants built their wooden churches on wheels.

Romania is now a Socialist State, the language is Latin-based and is thought to have been part of the heritage of the Roman Empire which occupied Europe more than 1,800 years ago.

Music

The music of Romania seems complicated compared with that of the countries in Western Europe; they are so fond too of elaborate ornamentations of a melody.

Their harmonies have a distinct oriental flavour, and frequent use of the interval of the augmented second; *accelerandos* and *rubatos* (see glossary). The dancer too must expect the step sequences to be quite at variance with the musical phrases. Some of the simpler dances have equally balanced music and movement, but more often regular music phrases will have irregular step and dance sequences and vice-versa. Also found is the dancer making a cross-accent with a step, namely — not following the musical accent — all very different from the Western approach.

Flutes, a form of bag-pipe, a special kind of lute called a *cobza*, an ancient type of pan-pipe are the most usual and traditional instruments found in the country districts. In Transylvania a small cymbalom called a *tambal* is found; this is not surprising as this region was once part of Hungary. The *tambal* has a relatively small range of notes; it is suspended by a strap which is worn round the player's neck.

The basic and most usual rhythm of the dances is in 2/4 time; but its interpretation is by no means simple.

Bartok, a native of adjacent Hungary, was inspired to write some lovely concert pieces based on Romanian melodies; and in conjunction with Constantin Brailoin did much research into the music of this country. George Enescu, born in 1881 was the composer, conductor, skilful pianist and violinist to whom much credit must go for popularising the folk-music of Romania. In this century Enescu divided his time between Paris and Bucharest: he founded the Academy of Music in Bucharest, but during his sojourn in Paris became a much respected teacher — among his skilled pupils the name of Yehudi Menuhin is probably the most famous.

Costume

Of all the Balkan States, the costumes of Romania are the richest in embroidery and design. The surrounding countries of Bulgaria, Hungary etc., have influenced some of the styles, but with all the many variations (each region having its own design) there is a very distinctive outline which makes Romanian costumes very different from other countries.

The basic foundation and a feature of the women's costume is the long-sleeved blouse with a rounded neckline, which is very beautifully embroidered, sometimes very heavily on the sleeves and down the front. Various forms of skirts are worn with a variety of different aprons. The striped double apron, one in front and one at the back, is very popular, as are the single aprons richly embroidered and decorated with sequins. Aprons woven in either horizontal or vertical stripes are to be found in many regions. Another feature of both women's and men's costume is the sleeveless, sheepskin short coat decorated with coloured embroideries and leather applique work. According to the region the *opinci* moccasin type of shoe is worn or a firm, low-heeled leather shoe.

The headdress usually consists of a long veil which can be draped and fixed in many different ways governed by age, fashion, area, status etc., or in some regions it is fixed to a little round black cap or *ciapsa*. Originally the veils were made of hemp or linen but later a soft cotton or silk was used. In Oltenia, young girls wear the veil loosely hanging down the back, sometimes reaching to the level of the hem, and when they dance it floats out behind giving a very graceful quality to the dancers' movement.

The men wear different styles of trousers, either loose or tight fitting and made of linen or wool. White shirts are worn outside the trousers with a belt or broad woven band fixed round the waist. Decorated sheepskin coats are worn and black sheepskin hats. In some areas neat, round, black felt hats with small brims are very popular. In the north in the Ouas region a small round hat of straw is worn; the hat is given to the man when he is a child and he never parts with it until old age. In this area the men also wear a type of loose bag or pocket which hangs across the chest by a strap. In some regions *opincis* are worn and in others the trousers are tucked into boots, especially in the Transylvania region.

Hemp, flax, cotton or wool (from the many sheep) are the main materials used. The elaborate embroidery found on the women's costumes gives a certain weight to the costume and although skirts are often full, the movement is restricted into the ground rather than developing a light quality.

Traditional Dances and Style

The *hora* is considered the most typical formation of all the Romanian dances. Thought to be of Greek origin, it dates from the time when the people living along the valleys of the Danube and the Carpathian Mountains came in contact with Greek culture. The *hora* has many variations of steps and melodies and is danced on all occasions as well as marking the stages of social life. When a young boy enters the *hora* it signifies he is approaching manhood, and for a girl, that she is reaching a marriageable age. There are *horas* for men, for women and for both sexes; they are danced at funerals, weddings, harvest; and a period of mourning is significantly brought to an end by once more joining in the *hora*. If, however, someone in the village has been unfaithful, broken off an engagement, been to prison etc., and tries to join in a *hora*, the dancers will stop until the culprit retires. The villagers can dance the *hora* all day, usually beginning with young people and then the circle will gradually become larger as the different age-groups join in. There is a Romanian saying "Life is short but the folk dance long". Danced in a circle or open circle the dancers link hands, elbows bent and dropped, the hands being about shoulder height. A rhythmic "jigging" movement is made with little sharp downward pulses.

Another very popular dance is the quick *Sirba*, usually danced by men in a line with their hands placed on their neighbours' shoulders, or the vigorous *Brîul*, in which the men hold belts or interlace arms in a "back basket" hold.

Alunelul is a well known dance, especially in Oltenia, and like the *hora* it has many variations and melodies. Each village has its own version, *Alunelul ca la Gorji* (*Alunelul* as done in Gorji), or *Alunelul ca la Bîrca* (. . . as from Bîrca) or *Alunelul Bătut* (. . . with stamps), etc.

Although circles, open circles and line dances are the most popular, there are also many couple dances, mostly to be found in Transylvania. It is thought that many of the couple dances were brought to other areas by the shepherds who crossed the Alps into the southern regions. In South Transylvania, the *Invirita* is a well-known couple dance, and this type of dance is performed either in a column or couples forming a double circle, one behind the other.

One of the oldest and most impressive of Romania's dances is the men's ritual *Călusari*. Believed to have magic properties it is performed on Whitsunday by an odd number of men, 7, 9 or 11 and is led by a captain, a standard bearer and a masked fool with sword and bells (not unlike the English Morris). The dancers carry long sticks and in common with other similar stick dances they perform with great energy and vigour. The dancers are supposed to generate special healing powers and it is thought that if young girls can get near to them during the dance they will remain healthy and beautiful. Anyone who is ill is placed in a position so that the dancers can jump over them in order to effect a cure.

At harvest time the girls perform the ritual *Dragaica* wearing wreaths of wild flowers. The style changes according to the regions and footwear, but the movement has a strong downward emphasis. The steps are kept near to the ground, the feet relaxed, and the quick, frequent changes of direction requiring relaxed knees and nimble footwork. The rhythm is often expressed with a shaking and jigging action in the arms.

Customs

Romania's large agricultural areas, the village communities and the life of the shepherds, have kept alive many of the customs, music, instruments and folk arts. Carpet weaving, pottery, embroidery and wood-carving (especially decorative wooden mugs) flourish.

The period of December 25th–January 6th, the 12 days of Christmas, is one of celebrations, when groups of boys go round the villages singing carols. According to the region, one of the boys dresses up as a stag or a goat and the local girls are expected to contribute something towards the costume; a scarf, a jacket, socks, blanket etc. Should a girl refuse or does not welcome the singers, then she is not allowed to join in the *hora* dances during the holiday period and so will be unable to marry that year.

New Year's Eve is celebrated by boys carrying a decorated plough through the streets greeting everyone they meet and wishing them a happy and successful New Year. They sing and mime the work of the harvest; the sowing, cutting, stacking, grinding and finally making the bread — a ritual to ensure a plentiful New Year. In some areas the boys crack whips, ring bells or imitate the roaring of a bull by the use of a special drum; all of these sounds are to ward off the evil spirits. Children in some villages actually make the furrows in the ground and at dawn on New Year's Day sow seeds in them. Very popular is the *Sorcoua*, a stick covered with large paper flowers which children carry through the villages.

In the Spring, a festival is held (especially in the north) before the shepherds take their flocks up to new pastures in the mountains, and in the autumn they will be welcomed back with special songs from the villagers.

As in other countries, Easter eggs are painted and decorated, and it is said that "when Christians stop dyeing their eggs red, the end of the world will be approaching'. In Romania the origin of this custom comes from a story that an old woman carrying a basket of eggs passed by Christ on the Cross and that some of his blood fell onto the eggs: they have been painted ever since in his memory.

Rain is all-important for crops and in a custom called *Paparuda* a young girl, or several girls will dress in leaves and dance through the village. Too much rain can be disastrous and if this should happen a clay doll, decorated with flowers and candles, is sent floating down the river or stream. It is thought that the doll is looking for the keys to heaven to lock the clouds and so stop the rain.

The end of the harvest is a time for celebrations and girls will make the traditional harvest wreath from the finest ears of wheat and corn. The wreath is then taken to the village to be admired and blessed for the recent good harvest and to ensure a plentiful one the following year. A branch of apples is cut from the tree and given to a young girl to count; the number of apples means the amount of years she has to wait until she is married (a similar custom is found in England but by counting cherry stones).

October is the most popular month for weddings; the livestock and poultry are well fed, the wines stored and the harvest gathered in. Before the wedding, the groom's mother places on a table a round loaf decorated with a lighted candle. On the arrival of the local men, who bring a small fir tree, the candle is then removed and the tree placed in the loaf. The tree is festooned with ribbons, paper flowers etc., and on top is placed an embroidered handkerchief. When it is completed then a *hora* is danced round it. The following day the fir tree is taken to the bride's house and in return she gives to the bearers a handkerchief, a necklace of gold coins and a wedding shirt, all for the groom (symbols of her love, wealth and fidelity). Guests at the wedding all receive embroidered handkerchiefs. On her wedding day the bride draws a bucket of water from the well and dips in a posy of sweet basil and then sprinkles the water in the direction of the four winds. The water that is left over is used by the village girls who sprinkle each other in the hope that they will be the next to be married.

Fir trees occur a great deal in folk-lore and design. In mountain regions, where a great many trees grow, one is always planted at the grave of a young man or boy who has died, the tree being decorated with flowers.

ENGLAND

An evenly balanced form of movement but with stronger emphasis in the Morris style; usually simple in technique but interesting and complicated in ground patterns.

General Background

England is the largest area of the British Isles, an island situated north-west of the continent of Europe. In the south the country is separated from France by the English Channel which, at its narrowest, is only 22 miles across. On the east coast is the North Sea with the various harbour and boat links with Scandinavia and the Netherlands. In the north, the country is bordered by Scotland, and in the west, Wales, the stormy Irish Sea separating it from Ireland. When the countries of Scotland, Ireland and Wales are collectively grouped together with England the country is then known as Great Britain, or the British Isles.

Although a small country, England has a diversity of landscape: hills, moors, lakes, and on the eastern side a large flat area. Throughout the country many magnificent castles and cathedrals are to be found.

The English are descendants of early invaders and colonizers from Europe and Scandinavia, with the Celts, Romans, Anglo-Saxons, Vikings all leaving their legacy in the names of places and words still used in the English language. King Canute was both King of England and Denmark. The last foreign invasion was in 1066 with the Norman Conquest and over 7,500 French words which were introduced by this nation and are still in use today.

As an island nation the English have always had a strong, sea-faring reputation and following closely on the voyages of other European countries, they began to acquire a vast Empire which, by the end of the 19th Century included 11 million square miles — a quarter of the globe. The English economy dominated world trade and finance with Queen Victoria ruling over an Empire "on which the sun never set". Due to this great expansion, the English language became (and still is) the international language of government, culture and commerce. The English left their mark throughout the world but other countries left few traces on the English themselves, apart from the introduction of tea from India and China in the 18th Century, now the national beverage.

The Empire also created the Lancashire cotton industry, which at the beginning of the 19th Century was the most important single industry in the world and which was the chief cause of the Industrial Revolution.

With the advent of World Wars I and II, the Empire gradually began to seek independence, the various countries only maintaining links with England through the Commonwealth Organisation.

England has a temperate climate with a population of over 55 million and over half live in or near the large towns and cities. Agriculture still occupies four-fifths of the land although few people are now employed on the land, England is however still known as "this green and pleasant land". Fishing has always been an important industry, as is coal, steel and wool.

In the past, England has had various religious persecutions, but has not had a revolution since the 17th Century or a civil war since the 18th which makes the country the most politically stable nation in the world.

Music

In olden times folk-dances were performed on the village green, in the streets or manor houses. Today, the music is supplied by excellent recordings of groups or bands composed of accordion, fiddle, double bass, piano, drums and guitar. The country people danced long before these instruments had been invented and it is important to know what instruments were used in order to assess the quality of sound — which in turn had an influence on the way people moved.

In early times the pipe and tabor provided the music. The pipe (wood-wind) was of a rather primitive nature, only having a few stops which resulted in producing a melody within a limited scale. The tabor was a small drum and created a simple form of percussion. Later the violin was the most usual and popular instrument used. The nature of these instruments resulted in single notes being played (not chords). When these tunes are produced on a piano, only a very simple accompaniment should be arranged in order to keep the rather even and unsophisticated style of the music. The phrases are usually quite regular in four or eight bars and with rather a repetitive melody. Although the melodies are simple they are often very beautiful and tunes such as "Greensleeves" are known throughout the world. The folk dance music was taken overseas with the dances; and melodies such as "Soldiers Joy" can be found in many countries. As well as the even phrasing, simple rhythms are found—usually in 2/4 or 6/8 time. The former (2/4) causing the dancer to give a more flowing quality to the movement, whereas the latter (6/8) often with dotted notes, resulting in skips and a more "bouncy" action. It is interesting to note the difference in the relationship of the dancers and musicians between country dancing and the Morris style. In the social approach in the country dances, the couples perform steps that are simple in technique and which can be performed to quite a wide variation in tempo, the dancers therefore following the musician who begins and ends with a chord, when they honour each other.

Morris dancers are trained to execute their more demanding technique, the dances being presented to an audience, the men wishing to display their virility and strength in the movements of elevation. The musician starts with a four bar introduction known as "once to yourself" so that the leader can approve of the speed. According to the amount of elevation the leader feels his team can acquire, he may call out "quicker" or "slower" the musician follows the dancers.

Holst, Herbert Howells, Arnold Foster are musicians and composers who have written works based on the English country style; but it is Vaughan-Williams who was chiefly responsible for the preservation and the research of Elizabethan and Jacobean folk-music. In 1932 his importance in this field was recognised by his appointment as President of the English Folk Dance and Song Society.

Costume

Although England is a country rich in folklore, dance and traditions, it has little to offer in the way of folk costumes.

With the revival of country dancing at the beginning of this century, a costume based on those worn by the peasants in the 18th and 19th Centuries was used for demonstration groups. The girls wore laced-up bodices, blouses, skirts with a pannier effect, bonnets or mob caps. The men wore the old country smocks, very similar in style to those found in France, Germany and other countries. A feature of the English smock was the embroidery on the yoke, shoulders and cuffs, known as smocking. From the colour of the smock it was possible to tell the region of the wearer and from the embroidery on the collar and side panels, the occupation or trade of the man. At the yearly hiring of farmhands at fairs, the farmers could read the symbols on the smocks of those waiting to be hired. In the 1930s a costume was evolved to give the dancers a new look and this consisted of a full, mid-calf length skirt in red, blue, yellow or green, which was worn with a neat fitting waistcoat and a long-sleeved white blouse. The men had either long dark trousers or breeches, a waistcoat and white shirt. A firm, low-heeled shoe was worn by both sexes, replacing the white canvas sports shoe (once a popular image associated with English Country Dancing).

The Morris costumes change from team to team according to the region and the different traditions. Basically it consists of white trousers, shirt, a pad of bells worn round the calf and a felt or straw hat decorated with flowers and ribbons. Added to this are various waistcoats, the *baldricks* crossed over the chest etc. The sword dance teams wear trousers or breeches, white shirts, jackets but no calf bells. Special costumes are worn for dances such as The Abbots Bromley Horn dance, or the coconut dancers from Bacup, Lancashire. The Bacup men blacken their faces, wear black jerseys, breeches, white stockings, clogs and have short white skirts. During their dance they beat little wooden discs, called nuts worn on the palms, waist and knees, which create a rhythm; a counterpart is found in Provence, France. The Morris men wear strong outdoor shoes which gives strength to the steps. An unusual costume is that worn by the "Cockneys" or those living in the east section of London. Known as "Pearlies", the girls' black skirts and jackets, and the men's black suits are covered with thousands of pearl buttons sewn on in elaborate designs. A Pearly King and Queen is elected and they can frequently be seen today at festivals, fetes etc., raising money for charity.

Traditional Dances and Style

Until the 19th Century, England was mainly an agricultural country but with the growth of the cotton and woollen industries, people migrated into the new towns and cities. It was during this time that many of the dances, songs and customs were forgotten. England has always had a tradition of dance, and in the time of Elizabeth I when both the courtiers and the peasants danced, the people were known as the "Dancing English". Many of the old country dances were also performed in the courts and manor houses but in a more refined way; the country folk also imitating the court dances.

English dances can be divided into four distinct groups:
a) Those performed by men and women and known as "country dances".
b) Those performed by men and are known as "Morris Dances".
c) Dances using swords or rappers and performed by men.
d) Solo dances such as Clog Dances and Hornpipes.

The country dances are based on fairly simple steps: walks, runs, skips, step-hops, polkas, rants, etc., but due to their simplicity they present problems in the execution, the evenly balanced movement and subtle quality often being lost.

The group dances consist of couples arranged in either circles, squares or longways sets, frequently with very interesting and quite intricate and complicated ground patterns. Many of the patterns made in the sets are thought to have originated from designs found on Celtic monuments and brooches.

A number of figures occur throughout the country dances; heys, siding, arming, stars etc., and in some duple, triple minor and longways sets, a progressive figure (i.e. couples changing positions in a set) is performed. The even quality in the music is reflected by the even arrangement of the step sequences, 8 gallops to the left is followed by 8 to the right, or 4 walks forward will have 4 walks backward, the sets always maintaining a balance in the patterns. During the time of the Commonwealth, dancing was discouraged and actually prohibited by the Quakers (although it still continued amongst the gentry); but with the Restoration of the monarchy, Charles II encouraged festivities of all kinds and the pleasure of dancing was re-established and enjoyed again by everyone. In the 17th Century when dancing was so popular at court, the country dances were collected and published by John Playford (who lived from 1623–1686). Playford was a music publisher and "vicar-choral" of St. Paul's Cathedral and so popular was his book The English Dancing Master (first published in 1651) that over the next seventy years he and his sons and nephews brought out many editions from their shop near St. Paul's Churchyard, London. Many other publishers followed his success and by the 18th Century country dances had spread to Scotland, Wales and Ireland. During the turbulent history of wars in Europe mercenaries, soldiers, and sailors travelled on the Continent taking with them many of the English dances. Merchants too on their journeys overseas selling their wares, have been responsible for instructing foreigners in the English style. The very popular style in the U.S.A. known as American Square originated from the British settlers. In fact the country dances were England's great contribution to the popular arts of Western Europe.

The country people kept the dances alive, changing the steps and figures to suit their own environment, the dances of the north being much more vigorous in style than those of the south. Those dances which did survive into this century were written down and collected by such people as Cecil Sharp, Maud Karpeles, Peter Kennedy etc.

Morris dances were originally performed by men who were specially trained to dance at the various solstices, usually to awaken the earth, generate the crops, dance magic into the ground or to scare away the evil spirits. The men carried handkerchiefs which they waved spreading the vitality which they had created from their vigorous jumps over the land. Sticks or slings (a kind of plaited rope) were also carried.

The steps of the dances are more intricate and stronger in elevation and attack than those of the country dance style.

The origin of the name Morris is uncertain, it is thought to have been derived from the Moors during the time when Spain was occupied by the Arabs. Spain and England had many close links and it is possible that the dances were introduced into England at this time. There is a strong similarity to the dances of the Basques and Northern Spain with those of Morris. In the Middle Ages, Morris dancing was performed mainly in the south of England, but like the country dances many became suppressed by the Puritans in the early 17th Century. It was only at the beginning of this century that Cecil Sharp revived the interest. There are over two hundred dances which have been collected and numerous teams and traditions (the execution of the steps differs slightly according to the regions). Most teams consist of six or eight men, with a Squire (leader), a Bagman (the treasurer), a Fool, Molly, Betsy or Maid Marian (a man dressed as a woman) and sometimes a Hobby Horse.

Sword dances are found mainly in the north of England, Yorkshire using the Long Sword and Northumbria the rapper, and have a similarity to many others in different European countries. The dancers hold the point and hilt of the swords and weave intricate patterns and designs. Between figures or at the end of a dance the swords are interwoven to form the Lock, Rose or Nut (the emblem of the English Folk Dance and Song Society). The steps are based on walks, and runs and are very different from the Morris style.

Clogs were worn in the northern industrial towns until the end of World War II, clog dancing developed by the workers in the mills during the industrial revolution as a form of enjoyment in often rather bleak surroundings. One of the famous dances was the Lancashire Hornpipe, with its intricate rhythms. A forerunner of step or tap dancing it has recently been revived with great success.

The Hornpipe is a very popular solo dance which is still performed today by naval cadets and consists of mimetic actions of a sailor's work on board a ship. Counterparts of this dance are also found in France, Russia and many other countries with strong naval traditions.

Customs

Islands and isolated districts usually have distinctive customs and special superstitions and this is very true of England. Most festivals stem from pre-Christian times and every country celebrates the seasons of the year but in different ways. England, at one time being predominantly rural and agricultural, the seasons or solstice played a very important role. Many of the customs also show the inheritance from the early settlers.

In January, Twelfth Night is celebrated by "Wassailing" (from the Anglo-Saxon word washal — to be hale or in good health). This custom was once prevalent all over England but now only found in the apple orchards and cider making regions of the west country. The apple, since the time of Eve, has had an important significance and in parts of Somerset a Wassail Queen is carried through the orchards pouring a libation into the fork of each tree. Dancing and singing takes place around the trees, cider is drunk and toast soaked in this drink is hung on the branches. Shots are fired, and pots banged in order to scare away evil spirits or awaken the gods of fertility. Plough Sunday (the first Sunday after Twelfth Night) ploughs are taken to the church to be blessed before being used to plough the first furrow of the New Year. A corn dolly made from the last stalks of the previous harvest is buried under the first furrow.

February 14th, St. Valentine's Day, was in pre-Christian times celebrated by the Romans honouring their goddess Juno who was symbolic of marriage. Later in the 3rd Century a martyred saint in Rome called St. Valentine was adopted by the early Christians who incorporated their festivals to coincide with the pagan ones. The giving of presents has always been associated with St. Valentine's Day, at one time in England it was customary for a boy to give a girl a pair of gloves; later these gifts became more varied such as perfume, silk stockings, embroidered garters and jewellery; now it is only a card!

The forty days of the Lenten Fast are preceded by Shrove Tuesday or Pancake Day. Shrove Tuesday was the day when people confessed or shrive their sins before Lent. The original idea for eating pancakes was to use up all the meat, butter and eggs which couldn't be eaten during Lent. Pancake races are held in many parts of the country today, the most popular being at Olney in Buckinghamshire in which the housewives run with their frying pans, at the same time tossing their pancakes in the air. The races were associated with a bell-ringing ceremony in the local church bidding the parishioners to a special "shriving" service. The story goes that one house-wife hearing the bells and fearing she might be late for the service ran all the way to the church clutching her frying pan!

Many countries hold different kinds of parties or feasts as a last "fling" before the restrictions of Lent. At one time Shrove Tuesday was always a holiday with horse-racing, a very rough type of football and cockfighting. Following a cockfight the scattered feathers were collected and stuck into a cork which was batted back and forth by players with flat pieces of wood — the origin of battledore and shuttle-cock or known later as badminton.

Mothering Sunday occurs in Lent and special family feasts were held, Sundays being exempt from the rules of fasting. Special fig-pies and Simnel cakes (from the Latin word simila-fine wheat, the cakes probably date from the Roman occupation) these are baked and given as a present by a young man to his prospective mother-in-law. Children on this Sunday make decorative bunches of wild flowers as presents for their mothers.

Maundy Thursday is a day associated with the giving and receiving of presents. The day commemorates Christ commanding his disciples to love one another, followed by the ceremony of washing their feet. Until the reign of James II, the monarch would wash the feet of as many poor people as his years. The custom began in the 14th Century by King Edward III who gave 50 pairs of slippers to the poor, his age being 50. Queen Elizabeth I gave cloth, food and money on this day and the present Queen continues the custom by giving "Maundy Money" to the poor of different parishes, the amount increasing each year.

Easter is a time of resurrection and rejoicing symbolised by the egg. In central Europe the art of painting eggs with intricate designs is of a very high standard. In England the eggs are usually dyed a bright colour by boiling them with flowers of anemones, broom, furze or whin; onion skins or cochineal. Egg rolling competitions are still a favourite game with children. A popular Easter figure is the rabbit associated with this season due to their fecundity. In Celtic times it was believed that the hare chased away the spirit of winter.

May festivals welcoming spring are celebrated in nearly every country. In England dances around the may-poles are still performed. The pole is decorated with flowers and ribbons and it was always a tradition to decorate the houses, sometimes under the cover of darkness, the choice of flowers being a comment on the inhabitant. Thorn was for scorn, lime for prime, pear blossoms for fair of face or character, holly or plum meant glum. A May Queen is usually elected, hobby horses appear, the local chimney sweep dances through the village and at one time the milk maids would dance with their pails decorated with flowers. The Helston Furry dance in Cornwall is a very well known dance still performed today.

On the 29th May, Oak-apple day, everyone used to wear an oak leaf in memory of Charles II who hid in an oak tree after the battle of Worcester in 1651.

At Whitsuntide the custom of "Well Dressing" once popular everywhere, survives only in Derbyshire, where the stone wells are decorated with flowers, moss etc., to depict a biblical scene. The next major festival was at harvest time; in pre-Christian times the harvest celebrations were held in honour of the goddess Ceres (her Roman name), and called Demeter by the Greeks. The last sheaf of corn cut was made into a "Corn Dolly" which was then brought home in a triumphant procession where it was given a place of honour at the Harvest Supper. The "Dollies" varied in shape and size according to the district, and were thought to contain the Corn Spirit and also ward off witches and evil spirits. The "Dollies" were then hung in the barn, farm-house kitchen, or in the church porch to ensure a good harvest the following year and then buried on Plough Monday.

Hallowe'en, the name comes from the old Celtic calendar, is a time for special indoor games and parties when apples play an important part (the games are thought to have originated from the Celtic "Winters Eve").

November is associated with Guy Fawkes, and today is a time for bonfires and fireworks.

Christmas and all the end of the year celebrations mark the ancient winter solstice which began on December 22nd. Unlike other countries, the festival of St. Nicholas is observed in England on December 25th and is an occasion for parties and giving of presents. The idea of Father Christmas or Santa Claus riding on his reindeer-driven sleigh, carrying gifts which he distributes down the chimneys and into the children's stockings hanging up from their beds is not new. It is thought to be based on the old Norse God Wodin (from which we get Wednesday or Wodin's Day) who drove through the sky scattering gifts. Burning the Yule-log and the use of candles is still popular today. Houses are decorated with mistletoe and evergreens; holly being symbolic of man and ivy the woman. Mistletoe was sacred to the Druids, and was the old Norse plant of peace, hence the custom of kissing under it. The day after Christmas known as Boxing Day was when the servants and tradespeople went round the houses collecting with their Christmas box.

So many of the customs are a reminder that their origins stem from the old fertility rites and for the continuity of mankind.

SCOTLAND

A dance form which has an upward emphasis; neat and controlled foot-work.

General Background

On May 1st, 1707, the Kingdoms of Scotland and England merged, their political identity to become the one Kingdom of Great Britain. Although Scotland is joined to England geographically and politically, it still maintains its own legal, educational and ecclesiastical systems as well as having its own bank notes and stamps.

The people are Celtic in origin, the name Scotland is thought to be derived from the Irish Celts (*Scoti*) who crossed over from Ireland in the 5th and 6th Centuries. The country is divided into the Highlands and Lowlands, the Highland Line crossing the country from Loch Lomond (just north of Glasgow) to Aberdeen. For most of Scotland's history, the two sections had little in common, the Gaelic speaking Highlanders of the north having a different language and outlook from the Lowlanders. Further divisions within both countries were caused by the Catholic and Protestant faiths, which led to much animosity against the Catholic Mary Queen of Scots. When not warring one against the other, patriotism and unity only became established when the Scots became united over the centuries against the English rule, or their wish for supremacy. In the 13th and 14th Centuries men such as William Wallace, who inspired the rousing song "Scots wha hae wi Wallace bled" and Robert Bruce, became National folk heroes.

Many of the words and place names reflect Scotland's rich background; in the north-east there is a strong Scandinavian influence; the north-west is more Celtic and Gaelic (which is still spoken), is the basis of many words, whilst others show a strong French influence.

In the early days of Scottish history there were three or more kings and numerous clans. Each clan had a very powerful chief (this is still the case) and members of the clan adopted the name; later when tartans became popular, each clan had its own special colouring and design.

Due to the difficult terrain and the problem of maintaining a living, many Scots sought work overseas. As far back as the 13th Century and the 1295 alliance with France, Scots fought as mercenaries in various armies, the King of France having a Scottish regiment. There were also links with the Netherlands and Scandinavia which resulted in an interchange of dances and music. In the 17th, 18th and 19th Centuries many emigrated to the U.S.A., Canada, Australia and New Zealand bringing with them their capacity for hard work. Throughout the world, wherever they have settled, Scottish music and dance flourish. Many countries now hold important Highland Games, have Scottish Country and Highland Dancing Societies and organise competitions and examinations, an example of the national spirit and sense of patriotism.

Music
On considering the music for Scottish dancing everyone's first thought and reaction is to their famous bag-pipe; however, dances existed long before the pipes.

Singing to accompany movement occurred in all countries in pre-historic times; but Scotland has a unique form of vocal accompaniment known as *puirt-a-beul* or mouth-music. This mouth music has a strange quality, it can still be heard today — usually in rather isolated districts; but particularly in the Outer Isles. No actual words are used — the "singers" make strange and rather unintelligible sounds with their lips; but producing a definite tune or melody with a strong rhythmic character, and with frequent use of the "snap".

The characteristic "snap" is a short note followed by a longer one (thus producing the rhythm of "quick-slow"). This quick-slow sound is heard in the music of other European countries — (particularly Hungary) but interpreted in a different way by the dancer. In Scotland the snap is most significant in their music. The different rhythms written in 2/4 and 4/4, and compound times of 6/8, 9/8 and 12/8 are used to accompany the various dance styles; but it is to the strathspey that the consistent use of the "snap" is found. The main interpretation of strathspey is—slower tempo—and it is usually written in 4/4 time; but its speed is the main concern of the dancer. The snap can be used in varying ways; but the most typical is when the emphasis is on the short note, and this occurring on the beat, and not before it.

The theory of the use of the snap and its interpretation is to help the dancer give elevation in the execution of the steps of a dance.

Before the bag-pipes existed the instruments used were violins or various kinds of wood-wind. The fiddler again produced the snap without much effort because with short upward and downward movements of the bow this effect or rhythm was easily obtained.

A simple bag-pipe with only one drone appeared in the early 13th Century; later a second was added and in the early 19th Century the third drone appeared and still pertains today. The three drones have very loud and sustained notes which form a background to the melody which is played by the fingers on the chanter and illustrating the frequent occurrence of the snap. The bag is held under the left arm-pit and is filled with air by the mouth before the piper starts an actual tune. (The reason for the strange, and rather peculiar sounds heard!) The air is then forced through the pipes by pressure from the elbow.

The rhythm of Scottish dance music has always been of great interest to foreigners; and in several European countries the word *schottische* appears in many of their named steps and dances.

Again composers such as Handel, Bach, Haydn, Mozart, Beethoven and Mendelssohn have been inspired by this characteristic style of rhythm and music.

Costume

The kilt is Scotland's national dress and is worn traditionally by men for Scottish dancing, Highland Balls, Highland Games or for everyday wear. The kilt developed from a long length of material which was wrapped round the body over a coarse tunic or shirt. The material was worn pleated round the lower part of the body and held in place by a belt, the remainder draped over the shoulder. In the extreme winter weather of the Highlands the material acted as protection and could also be used as a blanket at night. By the mid-18th Century the lower half had become a separate garment or kilt, the upper part becoming the plaid. The kilt contains about 16 yards of material and is pleated across the back, the front section being flat. Correctly, it should just touch the ground at the front when the wearer kneels. At one time a new kilt would be buried for six months in a peat bog or soil to give it a weathered look. The texture and weave of genuine tartan cloth was such that it could survive in all conditions and last for many generations. The kilt having no pockets, a sporran is worn across the front suspended from a belt.

In most countries it is the women who display the finest and most elaborate costumes, but in Scotland it is the men, the women having no definite dress. For everyday wear, the man wears a tweed jacket, kilt, tie, sporran and thick brogue shoes. For evening wear he wears with the kilt a velvet Dress Doublet, either green, blue or black with a lace jabot or a black coatee.

For Scottish country dancing, the man wears either the day dress or for a ball the evening version. The Official Board of Highland Dancing recommends the correct type of dress to be worn for competitions and for the man this is based on the evening dress but with black Highland pumps, and a woollen Balmoral bonnet or Glengarry (a type of forage cap) on his head.

For an informal dance the woman would wear a short full skirted dress with a draped plaid but for an important occasion it is usually a long white evening dress. The plaid is worn crossed over the right shoulder unless you are the wife of a chieftain or colonel, or the eldest daughter of an important and major family, then it is on the left. For Highland dancing the girl wears a kilt and a coloured jacket over a white lace-fronted blouse. A Balmoral type of bonnet can be worn. She is not allowed to wear a *skean dhu* (a small dagger), a sporran, belt, stocking flashes, a Glengarry bonnet or bows in the hair. For dances such as Scottish Lilt etc., a special costume called a Flora is worn which consists of a full skirt made of a light material in a tartan, a laced up bodice and a white blouse with half sleeves.

The Scots also perform a type of Irish Jig (inherited from the many Irish who settled in Scotland) and the costume is based on green skirts and petticoats for the girls, and knee breeches and jackets for the men.

Traditional Dances and Style

The dances of Scotland are divided into two styles, the Country and the Highland. The Highland dances were originally performed by men and were executed by the various clansmen and warriors to celebrate victory in battle, or perhaps like the pyrrhic dances of ancient Greece they developed strength of foot, limbs and co-ordination.

The dances stretch back into antiquity for the Romans reported having seen the Caledonians (the name they gave to the Scots) dancing wildly around and over their swords which were in a vertical position, the points thrust into the ground. The swords are still used but are now laid on the ground in the form of a cross, as in the Sword Dance, the dancer executing steps over and around them. The Lochaber and the Argyll Broadswords also use swords, but the cross is formed by the four swords of the four male dancers. The Highland Fling, a man's solo, was thought to have been danced on the targe or shield of his opponent, the dancer therefore keeping on one spot. With the defeat of Bonnie Prince Charlie by the English in 1745, the Highlanders were forbidden to wear the kilt or play the bagpipes and were forced to adopt trews or trousers. Trews were then worn by the clansmen, but they longed for the freedom of the kilt. From this historical incident, the dance Seann Triubhas (The Old Trews) was evolved, a solo in which the man shows his dislike of the trews. In 1782, with the repeal of the Act of Proscription, there was an immediate development for everything Highland, music and dance flourished, the Highland Games established etc.

The various pipers and dancing masters attached to the 20 or more Highland regiments began to develop the dances in a highly competitive and technical fashion with new steps and dances being created. Girls also began to study the Highland dances and dancing masters created especially for them — dances such as the Scottish Lilt, Blue Bonnets, Flora Macdonald etc., all in a Highland style and less demanding than the men's rather exacting and strenuous solos. The soft Highland pump allows the dancer to stretch the feet, and dance on the 3/4 point of the foot, the heels seldom lowered. The flat panel of the kilt and the sporran placed in front necessitated a turn out to the legs.

In Highland dancing the man can raise his arms, level with his head, imitating the antlers of a stag, the stag being an ancient symbol of manhood. In the dance the Reel of Four, the two men setting and turning one another represents two stags battling for the attentions of a doe.

The Country Dance was purely a social form and the various circles, longways sets, squares etc., were danced at weddings, *ceilidghs*, a *kirn* or "harvest home" to celebrate the completion of the harvest and annual balls given by the lairds for their tenants.

Many of the old figures and patterns are based on ancient Celtic origins, the cross, the clockwise or sun worshipping direction (to move to the right was *widdershins* or the witches way), chains etc. The oldest pattern is the Reel of Four thought to be linked with an ancient emblem found near the Standing Stones on Orkney.

Scottish dancing was very much frowned upon by the Scottish Church who associated it with witchcraft and the powers of darkness, but the Catholic areas were much more lenient and dancing was accepted.

During the 18th Century, country dances flourished, the dancing masters often naming the dance after a rich patron, a particular event, person, place or house. Dances from England also crossed the Border, Scottish soldiers brought back steps and figures (and also taught the Scottish dances overseas), and a certain French influence was introduced through the Court of Mary Queen of Scots and the connection with France.

There are three major types of dances, the Reel, Jig, and Strathspey. The word Reel referred not only to the dance rhythm, but could also mean a social gathering for dancing or to describe an interlacing figure such as a Reel of Three. The Strathspey is a slow dance and special steps are used to suit the tempo. It has been suggested that the musicians and dancers in the Spey region took all the reels at a much slower speed which in time developed into the Strathspey dances.

The Foursome Reel is a dance which can be danced by four men in a Highland version or in the ballroom in couples.

During the country dances ladies hold their skirts and the men have their arms at the sides and raise them only when they are performing any Highland setting step (Eightsome Reel etc.). Ladies never lift their arms.

Customs

With Scotland's Celtic background and the close link with Ireland, many of the customs show a similarity. The Highland people have a strong belief in changelings and fairies, a fairy being a guardian of one particular family or clan. In the castle of the MacLeods on the Isle of Skye there hangs a Fairy Flag which when waved in times of trouble will protect the family (it has so far been used only twice). A special fairy also acts as guardian over the Grants clan. Young children and babies are always susceptible to fairy lore and until a baby sneezed it was thought to be under the fairies' control. A weak, dark, undernourished baby is thought to be a fairy child. In some areas of the Highlands, a new born baby is placed as near as possible to the peat fire, if it was a changeling then it would vanish "up the lum" (chimney), the hearth and chimney being the abode of the "little people". Sometimes a ceremony called *saining* or blessing is carried out when the child is put into a basket of provisions and carried 3 times round the chimney. Alternatively, a lighted candle is carried round the bed 3 times, and a Bible and some food placed under the pillow. To protect both the mother and child the words "May the Almichty debar a' ill frae this 'uman, an' be aboot her, an'bless her an' her bairn", are said. At weddings in the Western Isles, an occasion for a great deal of merriment and dancing, the bride would suddenly disappear from out of a set, her place being taken by one of the bridesmaids. The groom as soon as he noticed her absence would be taken to her by the men, the idea was to cheat the local fairies who are particularly active and not unknown to spirit away brides on their wedding nights.

At Lowland weddings it is the custom to serve a fowl at the meal, the bride being given the small side-bone called "hug-me-close" a sign that she and her husband will always be happy together. Also at weddings the bride will give to all the guests "favours" which are the figures and decorations from the wedding cake.

Witches have also been very prevalent in Scotland, James I of England who was also James VI of Scotland, blamed them for causing such a terrible storm when his future wife Anne of Denmark sailed from Scandinavia to Scotland. For protection against witches a twig of rowan was always carried in a pocket or purse and branches of the tree placed over the doors, in the stables and byres. Crosses made of rowan twigs were placed in the cow stalls, fixed round the animals' necks or hung over a baby's cradle. Hallowe'en or the Celtic New Year is celebrated with bonfires. At one time every family built a fire and each member threw into the ashes a white stone marked with their initials.

Next morning, if the stone was missing then this was a bad sign that they would not see another Hallowe'en. At Balmoral during Queen Victoria's time an effigy of an old witch was always burnt on the traditional bonfire.

In Scotland, New Year's Day is celebrated and is considered more important than Christmas. The eve of the New Year is known as Hogmanay, a word which may derive from an old French custom called *hoguinana* or from a type of oatcake for which the children would beg on New Year's Eve. The first person to enter the house after midnight or "First Footing" should be a man, but if he was flat footed, lame or with a squint, then he was the bringer of bad luck. For good luck the "First Foot" carries a piece of bread or cake, and a lump of coal or peat to ensure food and warmth. For happiness he brings drink and for wealth a coin or salt. At one time people were paid in this vital commodity, the word salary deriving from the latin word *sal* — meaning salt.

Scotland's Patron Saint is St. Andrew, one of the twelve Apostles. The Saint's relics were brought to Scotland by St. Regulus who was shipwrecked at the place now called St. Andrews. Considering himself unworthy to die on a Cross of Christ he was crucified on an X shape, the emblem now on the Scottish flag. The Thistle, Scotland's other emblem is said to date from an incident at the battle of Largs (1263) when one of the barefooted enemy advancing in the dark trod on a thistle. The cry which he let out alerted the Scots and the day was saved. This incident is also said to have happened against the Danes.

IRELAND

The style in both forms has precision; but the step dancing having a stronger emphasis.

General Background

Known as the "Emerald Isle", Ireland is situated on the west coast of Britain with the Irish Sea separating the two countries.

It is a country of great beauty, very green, which gave rise to its name, and also containing many lakes, hills and mountains. The Irish people are very warm hearted and charming and have a very different outlook to life from those of their neighbours across the water in England.

The majority of the people of Ireland were of Celtic origin, who remained for many centuries untroubled by outside invasions. The Romans who had conquered most of Western Europe never crossed into Ireland and the people and the country, very uniquely, developed with a strong Celtic background. Later, the conquering Vikings sailed in their long boats from Scandinavia and founded settlements which eventually became Dublin, Wicklow, Wexford, Waterford, Cork and Limerick. The first invasion from England began under the Normans and Henry II, and so commenced a long series of conflicts lasting until the present day. The Normans were followed by the Tudors, Henry VIII being also King of Ireland, then the Stuarts. It was during the reign of James I, that in 1608 the land in the six counties of Ulster in the north was given to English and Scottish farmers with their strong Protestant background. Oliver Cromwell also brought his armies to Ireland to quell a great deal of unrest. It was only in 1921 that southern Ireland became Eire and the north remaining part of England.

St. Patrick, the Patron Saint of Ireland, introduced the people to Christianity in the 5th Century and who said that he "found Ireland all heathen and left it all Christian". Roman Catholic is the main religion with a following of 90% of the population, the Protestant minority living mainly in the north. The southerners have a soft, lilting quality to their voices, Gaelic still being spoken. The northerners have a harder tone with a strong affinity to the Scots. Villages in the north tend to be more formal in appearance, perhaps reflecting the Scottish Protestant tradition, those in the south are much more carefree in appearance.

Potatoes were at one time the main diet for the majority of the peasants and when a famine occurred in 1845–46 over one million people died of starvation. It was during this time that thousands of emigrants left for England and America.

Music

The music of Ireland is simple in rhythm and regular in phrasing. The time signatures are 6/8 or 9/8 for the jigs and 2/4 or 4/4 for the reels and hornpipes.

Not surprisingly the harp, like their neighbours the Welsh (also of Celtic origin), features most prominently in the history of their music and use of instruments. Many countries in Europe have different forms of bag-pipes, and among the Gaelic speaking people they have existed since the 11th Century and have always been most popular.

The Irish bag-pipe however differs considerably from the Scottish. The Scots have to keep the bag filled with air by blowing into it with their own breath, whereas the Irish have small bellows under the left elbow with which they pump air into it. The Irish bag-pipes are not nearly as powerful in sound either as the Scottish, nor does the significant rhythm of the "snap" occur.

Today the fiddle is used everywhere; also very popular is the melodian a form of concertina which was invented by an Englishman in the first half of the last century.

Many Irish folk-tunes have been collected by: P. W. Joyce, Sean O'Boyle, Francis O'Neill, George Petrie etc., and are obtainable throughout the Irish Folk Dance Society.

Costume

Life for the Irish peasant was not easy and clothes were very simple and hardwearing. Many people went bare footed or wore primitive shoes made from animal skins. The climate being damp, both men and women wore the thick, heavy cloaks or brats. These garments had an attached hood which could easily be pulled over the head on a cold day or in a sudden downpour. In the 17th Century these cloaks were worn all over Ireland by rich and poor alike. When a cloak was not in use it could be thrown back over the shoulders, which could have contributed to the slight backward lean found in the body when dancing. A mother would present her daughter with a new cloak on her wedding day and this would be kept for special occasions, the old one still used for going to market.

The women's costume worn for a *Feis* was evolved fairly recently and was designed to show the neat footwork and leg action found in the step dances. The dress incorporates certain rural features such as the cloak which has now become very short and is only worn for decoration. Each school or team of dancers have their own variation and colour of dress. The dress has long sleeves, a high neck and a full short skirt well above the knee. The collar and cuffs are made of Irish lace. Black stockings or short white ankle socks are worn.

The men wear a saffron or green kilt with a jacket, white shirt and a plaid attached to the left shoulder. Socks match the kilt or jacket. Unlike the Scots, the man does not wear a sporran with the kilt, as the movements of the legs in Irish dancing are taken straight forward rather than turned out.

Traditional Dances and Style

There are two styles of dancing in Ireland, the "country" and the "step". At all social events: weddings, funerals or wakes, *ceili* (the Gaelic word meaning a gathering of neighbours), etc., the country dances are performed, whilst the more complicated and technical step dances are executed for demonstration purposes or at competitions.

Music and dancing in Ireland has always been very popular, mainly due to the isolation of many of the villages and communities. Travel was difficult and mainly undertaken on foot, the people were poor, there were no halls in which to dance so social gatherings took pl ace at the crossroads, on a grassy patch (weather permitting) or in kitchens and barns during the winter. In the second half of the 18th Century professional dancing masters travelled throughout the country and it was during this time that dancing really began to be developed. The dancing master would visit a village and stay for about six weeks, usually with the local farmer and use his kitchen or barn for his lessons. The first step to be taught was the "rising step" in the jig or the "side-step" in the reel. For the pupils who did not know their right foot from their left (a universal problem) a piece of straw and hay were fixed to the pupil's shoe and the dancer would be prompted with "hay foot" or "straw foot". The solo dances required a great deal of practice and those who mastered the difficult steps (frequently created by the teacher), were much admired and asked to perform at gatherings. These step dances would be performed on the top of the table, or on a trap or half door taken off its hinges and placed on the ground.

For those not so proficient in step dancing, then the set figure, pattern or round country dances were taught, many of these being devised by the dancing master, each teacher having his own set of dances.

The step dances include single, double and treble jigs, slip jigs, reels and hornpipes, and can be danced as a solo or in couples. Today dancers wear a soft laced up pump, a light walking shoe or, if dancing the hornpipe, a buckled shoe. The dances, such as the hornpipe, which use a shoe, are usually referred to as heavy dances. The dancers are no longer limited by table top space and therefore travel very much more. The country dances are mainly reels and jigs and feature intricate patterns, said to reflect the Celtic and Viking designs found on the Tara Brooch and other metal work.

Longways sets, two couple sets, round dances and square sets are very popular with many of the dances having a repeating chorus or "Body" between each figure. The square sets are thought to have been introduced by soldiers returning from fighting in Wellington's army in France.

The style of dancing, especially the step-dances, is controlled with the upper body rigid, the movement coming only from the hips downwards. The dancing masters discouraged any arm movements, perhaps because the steps were complicated enough without having to think about use of arms. A good step-dancer was expected to be able to balance a pan of water on their head and not spill a drop, which necessitated the leg action being kept well underneath the body. The country dances have the same style but arms are used in various holds, steps are small and the legs not lifted so high. The smaller steps and the weight slightly back over the heels makes all the sets, figures and holds much more compact compared with the English and Scottish Country dances.

Customs

The very strong religious background of the Irish plays an important part in their customs, many of them being linked to the various saints. One of the most popular saints, known throughout the island, is St. Brighid (Patron Saint of cattle and dairy work) which is celebrated on 1st February. On this day St. Brighid crosses are made of twigs, straw or rushes and are hung up in the house or stable to honour the saint and gain protection. On the eve of 1st February a ribbon, a piece of linen or cloth known as "St. Brighid's Ribbon" is left on the step or windowsill so that when the saint passes by in the night it will be blessed. The "Ribbon" is then used for a variety of reasons, it is hung in the barn or tied round the neck of an animal who is sick, it helps to cure toothache, head aches, and all manner of pains, it is worn by fishermen and all who go to sea and is always carried by anyone migrating to another country.

St. Patrick's Day, 17th March, the Patron Saint of Ireland, was always observed by making similar crosses to those of St. Brighid, but now this custom has been replaced by wearing the shamrock, the Emblem of Ireland.

The first Sunday in Lent is known as "Chalk Sunday" and it is when children mark large white chalk crosses on the backs of anyone who is unmarried.

Midsummer fires, as in other countries, are very popular, the embers being collected and used as protection for the cattle and the home.

An old pagan festival known as "Puck Fair" is held every August at Killorglin, Co. Kerry. A goat is chosen as "King Puck" and after being decorated and enthroned is carried round the village accompanied by a young girl chosen as the Queen and who has the honour of crowning the goat.

At Hallowe'en in some regions, a single man will spread ashes or seeds across a quiet country lane and then watch to see who will be the first girl to cross the line; she will then be destined to become his wife.

Christmas was the traditional time for the "Wren Boys" when on St. Stephen's Day, 26th December, boys would carry a dead wren round the village, stopping at various houses to sing and beg for money to "bury the wren". A custom found in Europe, the wren was thought to have betrayed St. Stephen by his lively chirping. Today the "Boys" carry a bunch of feathers or ribbons tied to an evergreen branch rather than the bird.

It has been said that Ireland is "the land of saints and scholars" and from very early times poetry, music and song have held an important place. There are numerous legends and stories and the people have a strong belief in fairies and the "Little People" or the "Wee Folk". When building a new house a stick or new spade is placed into the chosen plot of land, if it has not been moved in the night by the fairies, then it is considered all right to start building. Many of the poets had the power through their writings to place a curse, known as "The Cursing Psalm" or *Salm na Mallacht*. A paper containing the verse would be placed in a rat's hole giving the rats instructions where to go, which was usually across the water. A verse left on some-one's door made the inhabitants dance continuously until he was finally summoned to remove the spell.

WALES

The dancing has an even quality with the emphasis being on pattern rather than intricate foot-work.

General Background

The Principality of Wales is situated on the western side of England; a region of roughly 8,000 square miles and with a population of 2½ million.

The Welsh are Celts, and were driven into this territory by the Anglo-Saxons (now termed English). The border between the two countries was fiercely defended until they lost their independence as a separate nation at the end of the 13th Century. Evidence of this resistance is seen today in the remains of Offa's Dyke and border castles. The retention of their own language shows a strong nationalistic tendency.

Of the six counties, the two most southern, Gwent and Glamorgan are the industrial regions and where the majority of the people live. Coal, iron and steel being the main productions and occupations of the people living in this area. The rest of the country is basically agricultural — sheep rearing among the hills and mountains being the main occupation of the farmers. Wales has spectacular scenery; interesting castles (some only ruins), pretty villages and one beautiful cathedral — St. Davids, and a long coast-line make it a popular place for holidays.

The revival of the nationalistic feeling and concern for local traditions, crafts and knowledge of the Welsh language has been of great interest and importance, particularly since the end of the second World War.

Because of the past history of the inhibitions and restrictions of a non-conformist religion — so many of the traditional dances have been lost, or not recorded; but now, through the efforts of the Welsh Folk Dance Society (founded in 1949) many dances have been revived. These dances may be seen today at many of their local festivals — which they call Eisteddfod.

Music

The harp, and the beautiful singing of the Welsh people are the obvious topics for consideration when discussing the music of this country.

The co-operation of the harpist and singer can be compared with the unity of the guitar player and flamenco singer in Spain. They complement each other, each contributing interesting improvisations in harmony and counter-point, and with the singers' spontaneous variations with the rhyming words of a song. Their choirs too are world famous.

Like many other countries, variations of a form of bag-pipe, wood-wind and stringed instrument exist. However, today the harp is still of paramount importance and is frequently used as the symbol of Wales, together with the red dragon, daffodil and leek!

Two Welsh melodies of international repute are *Ar Lyd y nos* (All through the night) and *Llwyn on* (The Ash Grove).

The importance of a special Eisteddfod which takes place every July in Llangollen is truly great and of international status. Many groups from other countries visit Wales and take part in the competitions, and so hear the music and beautiful choirs of the Welsh people. Bardic festivals too, take place annually when music and poetry is presented in competitive form by people from the surrounding district. The intonation of their language has a musical quality.

Costume

The present day costume is not old in design but was evolved in the 19th Century and based on those worn in the 17th and 18th Centuries. The women's costume consists of a dark coloured over-dress, the skirt being open down the front and folded back to show a bright underskirt or petticoat. Additionally a large blue, grey or checked apron, a white blouse, a shawl and a neat white cap or bonnet trimmed with frills and tied under the chin is worn. For outdoor wear a tall black beaver hat is worn over the frilled bonnet. Wool and flannel (from the Welsh word *gwlanen*) is used extensively for the overdress and underskirt.

The men wear dark-coloured breeches, a waistcoat and a white shirt, buckled shoes and white stockings are worn by both men and women. The shoes now replace the Welsh clogs which had wooden soles and leather uppers.

Traditional dances and style

Apart from a few dances recorded by Playford, Walsh and Maud Karpeles, very little detail is known about their traditional steps. A type of flat polka or skip change of step and other simple steps common to the English country style are the basis of their dances. Mention too has been made of clog dances, and a form of Morris dance called *Cadi Ha*.

The Puritans and the Ministers in the non-conformist chapels were most strict in their condemnation of the wickedness of dancing and it was prohibited for over three hundred years. It is known that traditional dances existed because of the Welsh names pertaining to the dance tunes that have been found: *Meillionen* (The Clover), *Aly Grogan* (Lumps of Pudding), *Rhif*

Wyth (a set for 3 couples consisting mostly of heys), The Llanover Reel was a courtship dance performed by one man and two women.

It is also recorded that girls performed a dance with garlands of wild flowers called *Dawns y Blodau*, another with small balls with ribbons attached called *Dawns y Pdau*, and in the *Rali Twm Sion* dance, they performed with bells.

However, history does record an interesting solo dance for women, performed with a large shawl, which mimed incidents from the battle called *Morfa Rhuddlan* in 1282, when the Welsh were defeated by the English and so lost their independence as a separate nation.

Customs

The Welsh being of Celtic origin have many customs also found in Brittany, the Isle of Man and parts of Scotland.

Seasonal customs are common to every country in Europe; but the one at Christmas called *Mari Llwyd* is still held today in South Wales. The horse (as in Hungary and Poland) has great significance among Celts. In this event the *Mari Llwyd* or Grey Mare is represented by a horse's skull placed on a long pole. A man carrying the pole is followed by a procession of villagers in strange costumes, some carrying brooms and among them Punch and Judy. The leader would knock on the door of the houses to bring the owners good luck. After entertaining them with song and dance, money was collected in a large ladle.

St. Valentine's Day in February is taken very seriously by the Welsh, when young men make elaborately carved wooden spoons to present to their girlfriends.

St. David's Day occurs on March 1st, a national holiday, as he is the Patron Saint of the country.

In summer in the north of the country, some villages still celebrate what is called *Cadi Ha*, meaning summer Kate, when they carry gorse and birch branches and perform a type of Morris dance with blackened faces.

Autumn and harvest time as in many other countries bonfires are made to scare off evil spirits before the rigours of a wild and cold winter.

The making of corn-dollies is brought to a very fine art in this country. Other crafts for which they are famous are wool weaving and tapestries; pottery and carving on slates.

FRANCE

The dances of France are performed with small precise steps.

General Background

After the U.S.S.R., France is the next largest European country. Situated on the western side of Europe it has three coastal boundaries, in the north the English Channel, the nearest point on the continent to the British Isles (only 22 miles from Dover to Calais). In the west is the long coastline onto the Atlantic which forms the Bay of Biscay, usually a stormy section of this Ocean, and in the south is the Mediterranean. The land frontiers are formed by the dramatic mountain range of the Pyrenees in the south which separates France from Spain. In the south-east and east, the Alps divide the country from Italy and Switzerland. Alsace-Lorraine is a region in the north-west and borders onto Germany, and finally there is a frontier with Belgium.

With such a large terrain there is a great range of climate, costume, customs and dances.

The French are a volatile and excitable nation, usually fairly small in stature. Their racial background can be divided roughly into three groups:
a) People with a Celtic tradition who mostly inhabit the north-west, Brittany being the main region.
b) A mixture of Latin-Teutonic and some Celt who live in the centre.
c) A mixture of Latin, and way back, Greek and Roman who dwell in the south.

It was the north-east frontier gap that made France easily accessible to the many different races, the country gradually becoming divided into numerous powerful kingdoms; Brittany, Flanders, Toulouse, Burgundy, Provence, etc. The Franks were one of the early settlers who came to dominate a great part of the country, the name France being derived from them. When the Angles and Saxons invaded England the Celtic inhabitants took refuge in Wales and Cornwall, many crossing the Channel to join the Celts in Brittany (then called Armour or Armorica). It was from these British immigrants that this region became known as Bretagne after Grande Bretagne or Great Britain, the present district of Cornouaille — meaning Cornwall. In the 9th Century, the Norsemen invaded France and settled in what is now known as Normandy. In 1066, William, a successor to the Viking King Rollo, led the Norman invasion across the Channel and made England a colony, not of France, but of the powerful region of Normandy. The Normans became assimilated into the English way of life and their independence away from their homelands resulted in frequent wars between the two countries. From the 4th–18th Century, the Kings of the Valois and Bourbon dynasties ruled the country, the most significant being Louis XIV. It was only when he came to the throne in the 17th Century that a national unity was established. In 1789 the French Revolution brought to an end the established way of life and disposed of the royal family and aristocrats. It was an event which not only changed France, but affected the whole outlook in Europe. Following the Revolution, Napoleon I came to power (1792–1814) and then from 1814–1848 Kings of the Bourbon and Orleans dynasties were restored to the throne.

In 1871 and to the present day, France was finally established as a Republic. During the Renaissance period of 12th–16th Century the arts flourished in France: music, painting, sculpture and dance (particularly at the court) became very important.

Various religious differences, especially between the Roman Catholics and the Huguenots resulted in many of the latter fleeing the country thus promulgating their cultural skills; and many settled in Spitalfields in London, a district which became famous for its fine silk work.

The occupations of the people are both industrial and agricultural. Their vineyards and wine-making are considered the finest in the world.

Music

Precision is the cogent word attributable to so many aspects of the French people: the way they dance and speak. The sound of an accented language must inevitably have an influence on the music accompanying folk-song. Music for folk-song and folk-dance are of the same quality.

In French music the intervals between the notes in a melody are small, and the melodic line is often very repetitive in its range and phrases.

The instruments used are much less heavy in sound and quality than those of their German neighbours. For example in Brittany the melody would be sung or played on the *bombarde* (a kind of oboe) and accompanied by the *biniou* (a form of bag-pipe). The *biniou* makes a drone-like sound; but not nearly as strong as that associated with the Scottish bag-pipe. The *vielle* (a type of hurdy-gurdy) is found in many regions especially the Auvergne; this instrument is played by turning a little handle with the right hand, whilst a small keyboard is played with the left. Once popular in Germany, Holland and England it is also found in Hungary, thought to have been brought to the different countries by local French bands and settlers. In Hungary the sound is harder, the French being more precise in quality. The popularity of the *vielle* developed from the fact that peasants had very little money with which to pay several instrumentalists. The sound from a hurdy-gurdy carried well outdoors and the player would often sing too; all that was needed for dancing. It has also been suggested that one or two players eat far less than a band, or if playing all the time have no time to eat at all! The small number of notes on a *vielle* restricts the range of the melody.

In a country as large as France instruments do vary according to the region, and the cornet, different types of wood-wind and drums are found. Musical instruments in mountain regions have much in common, and in Provence, the Basque country and Catalonia the "one-man band" is very popular. One man plays the melody on the pipe using his left hand while at the same time strikes a little drum (attached by a cord round his neck) with his right hand. The tunes are often written in a 6/8 time which gives a light skipping quality to the dance steps. The proximity to another country has an effect on musical styles and instruments. Alsace bordering on to Germany uses the occasional brass instrument; but in not quite such a harsh manner as their neighbours.

Throughout France the music is simple in harmony and usually of a brisk and light quality.

Many composers have written music based on folk themes including Massanet, Faure, d'Indy, Grovley, Ladmirault, Froberger, Bizet etc.; but it is to Bourgault Ducondray that the French owe the research and establishment of folk-music, in the same way the English owe a similar debt to Vaughan Williams.

Costume

French costumes, like the music and dances, are neat and simple in style. In a country as large as France there are numerous variations, but all show a very practical style devoid of any over-elaboration.

Women's skirts are full, calf-length (allowing for plenty of movement), the material being either of a plain colour, floral, patterned, striped or having one or two broad bands around the hem line when the skirt is plain. Bodices are usually laced up the front and worn with long or short-sleeved blouses. It is thought that the bodice was first derived from one worn by Queen Marie of Anjou in the 15th Century. In some areas long-sleeved, tight jackets or well fitting dresses replaced the bodice and blouse styles. Aprons also vary from white, coloured, made or edged with lace. Many of the costumes are accompanied by delightful shawls or fichus, some being made or trimmed with lace, others of a plain or patterned material, and several having a fringed edge. The different styles of hats and bonnets are a distinctive feature of the women's costume; each region or village having its own particular design. The hats can be small and neat, to the more elaborate which are thought to have been based on the *Hennin* once worn by the ladies in the late medieval period. These head-dresses are made from starched muslin, fine linen and lace and although often very large in size, are light in weight, which makes the turning of the head quite easy. Wooden sabots were once worn in most areas, being replaced on Sundays and festivals days by a black outdoor shoe. In the south, rope soled, canvas topped *espadrilles* or a light weight slipper replace the heavier sabot of the north and central regions.

The men's costumes do not show such a wide variety of styles as the women. Very popular are the loose fitting workers' smocks, often blue in colour, but white in Provence and striped or checked in Bresse. In several regions the costume is based on a style consisting of knee breeches, waist-coats, jackets and shirts but with many variations on this outline. Peaked caps, berets, top hats, straw hats, flat brimmed felt hats, and a type of pull-on stocking hat are all popular in the various areas. Sabots were once the main footwear, apart from the *espadrilles* of the south.

Traditional Dances and Style

Due to the small intervals in the music the range of movement in the steps is also kept small. In the central and northern districts sabots were worn (in some areas they are still the normal footwear) which restricted the width of a step, the feet being kept under the body.

Precision in movement is the characteristic feature often emphasised by heel and toe actions of the foot. Many of the dances are quick and the dancers travel with great speed and nimble footwork covering the ground well.

France has always had a great tradition of dance (the Paris Opera Ballet is the oldest established company in the world) and Paris acknowledged as the artistic centre of Europe. In Medieval times the various circular Branles, and the Farandole with its different figures became the basis for both court and peasant dancing. In court circles these two dances developed, the Farandole eventually culminating in the 16th Century Coranto, whilst the Branles lasted at the French court into the 18th Century, although in a very different form. In folk dancing these dances continued very much in their basic form and are found not only in France but in many parts of Europe. There was, however, an exchange of dances between the court and the peasants and vice versa. Dances such as the Gavotte, Bourrée, Rigaudon, Gigue and the later Quadrille all had counterparts amongst the peasants or were based on peasant dances. The famous dance the Minuet developed from the *Branle de Poitou*, as did the Waltz stem from the *Landler* of Germany and Austria, and the *Polka* from Bohemia.

Throughout France there are numerous couple dances, circles and chains, many incorporating interesting patterns and figures. Also to be found are dances based on work themes, although several of these now only exist as children's games. Dances with actions associated with bell-ringers, woodcutters, bakers, spinners, weavers, and particularly harvesters need care and observation. There are also many dances in which "props" are carried such as decorated half hoops or arches (Les Treilles from the Languedoc and Provence), ribbons, sashes, lace handkerchiefs, a broom, while there are men's dances, not unlike the English Morris, in which swords, sticks and coconuts are used and a hobby horse being a central figure.

Each region has its own particular style and group of dances; the climate, terrain etc., influencing the interpretation. Brittany in the north-west corner of France, is surrounded by water on three sides, the dances therefore show very strong links with the sea. Each village has its own variation of a *Branle*, called in Brittany — a *Ridée*, which simulates the movement of the waves. The action of the waves is also reflected in the arm movements which are small and neat swinging up and down from the elbow (rather than from the shoulder as in English Morris). In some circle dances with a three beat rhythm a cross-accent is developed, the arms lifted up and down in a rhythm or count of two and the feet moving in a count of three. In this region Gavottes are danced but in a line of four, a feature being the *paz dreo* step which gives to the line a forward and back action reflecting the movement of the waves.

The Auvergne in Central France is famous for its *Bourrées*, a dance from which the ballet step *Pas de Bourrée* owes its origin. Unlike the *Bretons*, the arm movements in these dances swing from side to side in a cross-accent as the dancers execute their *Bourrée* steps.

In Provence, southern France, the famous *Farandole* is found based on the ancient Greek myth of Theseus and the Minotaur. The patterns in this dance represent the intricate forms of a maze. The Greeks once occupied this region of France and their ancient method of dancing the *Farandole* followed the anti-clockwise ground pattern still used in Greece today. Due to its popularity and inclusion in the French courts the pattern became adapted to the clockwise or sun-wise direction of Western Europe. This chain-dance was probably known in Crete during the Minoan civilization (1400–1200 BC) over three thousand years ago, and together with the circle dance formation (as in the English Country Dance — Sellenger's Round) are the oldest of all Western dance forms. The steps, as in other parts of France are precise but in Provence they have a light and almost balletic quality.

Customs

Due to the size of the country and the variety of the landscape there are numerous festivals and customs, many connected with the local industries or crafts such as wine making, cheese, lace and embroidery. Flowers also play a very important part in both the dances and customs. Special festivals are held when the flowers, and especially roses, are gathered for the making of perfume, a very prominent industry in France. Flowers are used to decorate half-hoops, baskets and on special occasions are made into garlands to decorate the fishing boats. Different kinds of fruit such as whortle-berries, cherries, hops, apples, grapes, strawberries are all honoured at different times of the year with dances, songs and festivities, even a *Branle* is danced round a cabbage or the root of a vine. In a mountain village in the South of France a *Fete de Fungi* is held when everyone collects the local fungi or mushrooms which are then cooked in the local wine. The person who finds the largest fungus gets a prize; the whole village then joins in a special dance. Sprigs of gorse, mimosa, almond blossom, lavender, lime, olives and branches of fir and vine are all used in dances and processions. A sprig of broom was always worn in the hat of Count Geoffrey of Anjou (his son Henry became Henry II of England). The latin word for broom is *planta genista* from which is derived "Plantagenet" — a line of succession which passed through 14 Kings of England. From early times, flowers have been used in courtship and in some areas it was the custom for a young man to place a *ramelet* outside a girl's house. The gift could be a bunch of flowers, a sprig of blossom or even an orange on a plate! If she wished to encourage him she would give him an iced cake.

Religion plays an important part in France, the majority of the people being Roman Catholic. As in Italy and Spain, the various trades and occupations are linked to a particular saint and their special days are occasions for festivals and dances. In Brittany there are numerous religious pilgrimages to the different saints, holy wells and fountains. These processions which are known as *Pardons* occur at different times of the year. The Holy Wells with their health-giving waters were at one time venerated in Cornwall and other parts of England (the custom is still maintained in the Well Dressing ceremonies in Derbyshire) but the pagan gods have now been replaced by Christian ones. In some *Pardons* the pilgrims still dance a *Ridée* round the well or fountain. One of the most popular of the *Pardons* is to St. Anne in the region of Cornouailles. St. Anne was mother of the Virgin and grandmother to Jesus so she is particularly favoured by grandmothers. There is a healing fountain dedicated to her and through various connections with the sea is much admired by sailors. St. Ronan, an Irish-Celtic saint, is associated with bells (he always carried one), Our Lady of Rumengol with songs, and St. Servais was protector of the crops and against cold weather.

The New Year begins in France with the young men giving to their girl-friend an orange into which a flower is set (called a "flowering apple"), he however has a long wait for her favour as only on September 8th will she give him a ribbon — if so inclined! In Alsace, between Christmas and Twelfth Night an old woman called "Berchta" (known by different names in other parts of Europe) comes around to see if everything is clean and tidy. Fresh straw is put into the barns and no flax or wool should be left on the distaff. On Twelfth Night pancakes are made, some being left on the table for her.

In Normandy on Twelfth Night a dance is performed round the apple trees, a similar custom to that found in the west of England, Normandy being well known for its cider and *calvados* (a liqueur made from apples).

Shrove Tuesday is the day when the straw man or winter is burnt. In Burgundy a mock funeral is held with the straw corpse pulled through the streets followed by his widow (usually a man–woman character). On Palm Sunday children make and decorate wooden sticks, sometimes with an orange stuck on the top or carry branches with sweets attached to them. The sticks or little trees called "Mays" (which resemble the Greek Thyrsus) are also made on St. Agatha's Day when they are planted in the fields to help fertilise the crops. On this day bread which has been blessed is kept on the kitchen chimney piece for good luck and prosperity.

May 3rd is the gipsy festival held at Saintes Maries-de-la-Mer, in the Camargue, when gipsies from all over the world gather to pay homage to their Saint Sarah or Sara. It was to Provence that Mary, the sister of the Virgin, Mary the mother of apostles John and James, together with Lazarus (who was raised from the dead) and his two sisters Martha and Mary Magdalene, fled after the crucifixion, accompanied by a servant, Sarah. The statues of two of the Marys and also of Sarah are carried out to sea in a boat, escorted by the Camargue cowboys or "guardians". Earlier in the year in Marseilles, small biscuits or cakes are made in the shape of a boat and called *navettes*, representing the boat in which the Holy Marys travelled.

As in other parts of Europe, St. John's Day or Midsummer is celebrated with bonfires, "if no fire is lighted, no sun will be seen through the coming year". The bonfires are decorated with wreaths, ribbons, roses and poppies and the children make posies of flowers which they singe in the lighted fire for good luck. Special flowers are associated with this day and "mugwort" is made into wreaths called "St. John's Girdle" to protect the corn from mice. In Poitou the girdle is worn against backache and in Normandy as a safeguard against thunder, thieves, and witches while in other regions they are placed over the door of the cottage or house.

Rogation Sunday sees the blessing of the crops, vineyards and animals. In some wine growing regions the statue of St. George has his feet washed in wine to ensure a good crop next year. If however it has been a bad harvest his treatment is not so kind.

The Fete of St. Catherine on 25th November, is celebrated by girls up to 25 years "the catherinettes" who had not yet married and who wear a special St. Catherine's coif. Very popular at one time in Paris when all the dressmakers had a holiday.

At Christmas time cribs are made and in Provence special clay figures called *santons* are made to decoraté them.Children put out shoes or *sabots* for the Christ Child or Father Christmas to fill. On Christmas Eve a fire or candle is left burning and food put on the table in case the Virgin Mary passes that way. On Christmas Day an extra place is laid at table in case any traveller should knock at the door, he is then invited in for a meal.

WEST

GERMANY

The dances of Germany are usually strong, boisterous and rather heavy in quality but with an upward emphasis.

General Background

Throughout much of its history, Germany was made up of a patchwork of various-sized kingdoms, principalities and grand duchies. In 1789 there were 1,789 separate independent units which constituted the Holy Roman Empire (the name given to the whole of the country). Until 1837 the King of England was also the King of Hanover, and up to 1864, the King of Denmark was also the Duke of Holstein and Lauenburg. Queen Victoria of England married her cousin, Prince Albert from Saxe-Coburg-Gotha. It was only in the late 19th Century that the first German Reich or empire was created to try and establish some form of unity and to link the various major and minor powers together. In 1933, Hitler became the *Führer* (the leader) and formed the Third Reich (intended to last for a thousand years). However, after only twelve years, and the horrifying events of the Second World War, the country was divided into zones occupied by the four major allies — the U.S.A., the U.S.S.R., Great Britain and France. The Soviet sector became the German Democratic Republic, and in 1949 the British, French and American Zones were re-organised into the German Federal Republic, with Bonn as the capital. In 1961, the Berlin Wall was built which not only symbolises a difference in ideologies between the Federal and Democratic Republics, but separates East and West Germany.

East Germany is bordered by Poland in the east, Czechoslovakia in the south, Germany in the west, with the Baltic Sea forming a natural frontier in the north.

The northern region is very flat and mainly agricultural, the most picturesque part is in the south with the Harz mountains and the Thuringia Forest. Dresden and Meissen (famous for their china), Leipzig and Weimar are the major cities now in this part of Germany.

West Germany is over twice the size of their Eastern neighbours and has four times the population. In the north it borders onto Denmark and the North Sea, with the Netherlands, Belgium, France on the west, and Switzerland and Austria in the south. It is a land of contrast which blends medieval hamlets, walled towns, romantic castles, lakes, mountains and rivers with flat plains and modern cities. In the old town of Nordlingen, the nightwatchman still calls the hours as he walks through the narrow streets. Both countries produce metal, chemicals and cars; the east specialising in iron, steel, crude oil and grain.

Music

The music of the German peasant has much in common with the Austrian; but it has a more strident quality due to their love of brass. Like many other European countries, the early instruments were the pipe and drum; but by the 19th Century every village had its own little band. These bands consisted of at least two brass instruments, if possible two or three stringed instruments and a clarinet; sometimes too the triangle and *glockenspiel* which is typically German. When singing accompanied a dance, it was called a *reigen*.

The accordion is of course a fairly recent acquisition; but very popular being easily transported by the player and with a tonal quality which carries well in the open-air.

The harmonies in the music are quite simple, and the phrasing usually regular. The first note of a phrase is well accented and called an *appel*; this may be a reflection of the rather military and well disciplined aspect of this nation.

Their great love of music is evident when one realises that nearly every town has its own opera-house.

Their tradition of great composers is very impressive, especially when one thinks of Bach, Beethoven, Handel, Haydn etc.

Costumes

West Germany can roughly be divided into the north and south, the costumes worn in the south (Black Forest and Bavaria) and the Rhinelands in the west are much brighter in their use of colours and design than those of the north.

The southern regions are mainly Roman Catholic and in common with other countries of the same faith, stronger colours tend to predominate. Bavaria is the largest state, occupying a third of the Federal Republic, and has been a separate monarchy for seven centuries until 1918. The people in these areas are inclined to have a more relaxed and easy going approach to life which is shown in their costumes and the softer pronunciation of the language.

The people in the north are very hard-working and have a sterner view of life. Protestant by faith, their costumes tend to be more sober in colouring using black, blues, greens and purples. Unlike the southerners, their accent is harder which perhaps reflects the flatness of the land as opposed to the mountainous regions of Bavaria. The women's costumes throughout the country show numerous ways of wearing bodices, skirts, aprons and blouses. Bodices can be quite plain or embroidered, trimmed with braid, velvet, buttons or ribbons. Skirts are usually full, sometimes pleated and often in a plain colour. Many petticoats are worn which allows for freedom of movement and acts as a modesty safeguard in some of the more vigorous turning and couple dances. Aprons are worn in most regions but tend to be plain in the north and flowered, braided or embroidered in the south. Red, yellow, blues and greens are the colours mostly used in the south.

Throughout both East and West Germany there are numerous types of hats which range from little bonnets, various types of felt hats decorated with ribbons, pom-poms, braid etc. There are also flat straw hats, sometimes yellow or lacquered white. In some regions the hats are tall, or made from ribbons, whilst others denote religion or whether married or single.

A firm shoe is worn with white stockings.

The men's costumes are similar in style to those found in other Teutonic countries; knee breeches, waistcoats, jackets, shirts and various types of hat according to the region. The knee breeches are often black or of a dark colour; in the south they frequently have embroidery on the front flaps and on the sides; but in the north they tend to be plainer. In Bavaria they are made of leather, the breeches often being replaced by leather shorts or *lederhosen*, which are common to both Germany and Austria.

Red is a popular colour for waistcoats, and they can vary from double or single-breasted, V-neck or high. Brightly decorated braces are found mainly in the south. One or two rows of silver or gold buttons fasten the many different styles of jackets and waistcoats. Black top hats or round felt or beaver hats with various sized brims are very popular and in the north a black tricorn is worn.

White or black socks are worn with silver-buckled or plain black shoes.

The areas of the Federal Republic which border onto Denmark, France, Holland and Switzerland have a similarity of style with those of their neighbours, whilst Poland, Czechoslovakia, the Baltic and Scandinavian countries have influenced the costumes now found in the German Democratic regions.

ASPECTS OF FOLK DANCE IN EUROPE

Traditional Dances and Style

The very different and contrasting geographical aspects of the country have produced many varied types of dances. In the north where the ground is flat the dances tend to be formal and are based on square formations with the popular chain, hands across, stars or mill figures etc. Many of these dances show a similarity to those of Denmark and Holland and reflect the popularity of the English Country dances which spread into Europe. Couple dances are found in all regions but when danced in the north they cover the ground more and are less exuberant than those of the Alpine area of the south.

In Central Germany the style of dancing tends to be stronger and more boisterous. Towards the south-west and the Black Forest region some of the dances have changing time signatures, the dance ending with a quick waltz or polka; other dances start at a medium speed and then the music quickens with the dancers following with runs, gallops, waltzes etc. In the mountain and Alpine regions of Bavaria the dances are very similar in style to those of Austria. In common with many mountain people, space is restricted and the dancers tend to confine their movements to turns and elevation rather than covering the ground. Claps, stamps, various types of turns, arm holds and positions are found. In many of the dances the girl dances in front of the man whilst he follows flicking her skirt, flirting etc.

There are very few of the old circle and chain dances to be found. These used to be danced round the spring or midsummer bonfires but with the very strict outlook of the Protestant Reformation, many of the dances were forbidden and eventually became forgotten.

The couple dances travelled into Germany via their neighbours, the waltz from Austria, the polka from Czechoslovakia (Bohemia), the mazurka from Poland. In the Catholic south they became very popular and gradually spread to other parts of the country. Many of the dances changed as they travelled and different names and variations were introduced. Several of the dances were taken into Holland and crossed over into Switzerland. Due to so many divisions among the nobility and their courts, the fashionable dances of the 18th and 19th Centuries (quadrilles, long-ways sets, mazurkas etc.) were extremely popular and in time also influenced the dances of the peasants. There are numerous dances which indicate the country of their origin by the name or steps (schottisch, mazurka, polka, rheinlander, waltz, gallop etc.).

Apart from the social dances there are also several guild dances, the Coopers who carry the half-hoop, the Cutlers with swords and the Drapers with flags.

At a wedding the bride would be blindfolded, and the unmarried girls dance in a circle around her; whoever she caught would be the next to be married. The bride also is expected to dance with all her husband's relatives as a token that she is accepted by his family. Three lighted candles are placed on the floor and they must dance round these without extinguishing the flames; if she succeeds then she will have a good marriage.

Customs

Germany has always had a long tradition of festivals, fairs, celebrations and customs. It is a country which inspired the Brothers Grimm to write their fairy stories, and for Wagner to compose his operas based on the legends of the *Nibelung*. The ballet *Giselle* is set in the Rhineland, Act 1 showing the wine harvest celebrations (still held in this region) and the famous legend of the Pied Piper is enacted each summer in the picturesque town of Hamelin.

Many of the customs have counterparts in other northern and neighbouring countries but with slight variations.

The preparations for Christmas begins with the making of an "Advent Wreath" using pine branches and four candles. The wreath is either hung from the ceiling with coloured ribbons or placed on a table, one candle being lit on each Sunday before Christmas.

On 4th December, St. Barbara's Day, special branches or Barbara twigs are picked and kept in the house hoping that they will bloom by Christmas. Germany is famous for its beautiful carved Christmas cribs, and the very popular "Christmas Pyramids", which are made in layers and revolve slowly, propelled by the heat from several lighted candles.

The 5th December, St. Nicholas' Day, is when the children receive presents and a shoe or boot is left out to be hopefully filled with sweets and gifts. On Christmas Eve before the tree is lit and before the family have eaten, the farm animals are always fed, the animals being the only ones who kept Mary and Joseph company during the birth of Jesus.

Germany is well known for its marvellous confectionery and at Christmas special biscuits, honey cakes, gingerbread houses (after Hansel and Gretel), logs and *Stollen* are made. The *Stollen* is a long shaped cake covered in white icing and represents the Christ Child wrapped in swaddling clothes.

Foretelling the future is a popular custom everywhere. If during the Twelve Nights from 25th December to 6th January a young girl throws her shoe into a pear tree 12 times, she will marry the man of her choice, should the shoe remain in the tree. On St. Andrew's Night, 30th November, if at midnight a girl throws her slipper over her shoulder towards the door, she will soon discover if she will be married that year if the toe is pointing towards the door. The peel of an apple thrown over the shoulder on New Year's Eve will give the initial of her true boy friend.

In some areas it is customary to throw peas at neighbours' windows on New Year's Eve or present them with an apple stuck with coins. A straw doll was often made and drowned in the river at midnight, and in some villages a girl would be chosen as the New Year Queen, if she failed to marry within the coming year she would be "an old maid". On the eve of Epiphany, water blessed in church is sprinkled around the home, stables, fields and animals.

Driving out winter and welcoming summer is celebrated by children making special decorated "Spring Stacks" with paper flowers, egg shells etc.

Easter is an important occasion with painted eggs, bonfires and the making of Easter wreaths and trees decorated with eggs. On Easter Saturday children make little nests of straw, moss and twigs and leave them in the garden so that the "Easter Hare" will know where to leave the eggs during the night. Children also make an "Easter Bird" or "Paradise Bird" or "Holy Spirit Dove", the body being an egg with feathers and ribbons added as wings, a head etc.

Daffodils or "Easter Bells" always decorate the house at Easter time. On St. John's Eve a girl will make a wreath and hang it on her front door; this is to let her boy friend know her answer. If the wreath is made with cornflowers it is "yes", but if of thistles it is "no".

"Topping out" is an important part of house building. When a house is partially built a Fir Tree in North Germany or a Wreath in the south is placed on the scaffolding and a good luck toast drunk by the builders.

HUNGARY

A dance form which has a strong rhythmic content with a downward emphasis and many turning and twisting movements.

General Background

Hungary — an inland state roughly in the centre of Europe has had a turbulent history of wars with the surrounding countries. To the north and west is Austria, north — Czechoslovakia, in the north-east corner a short frontier with the U.S.S.R., to the east Romania, and to the south-west Yugoslavia.

The Hungarians have always been a war-like nation, and their character is of a very purposeful quality. The Ottoman Empire was not only of great significance in the history of the Balkan States: the Turks penetrated into central Europe, and were not driven out of Hungary till the Austrians became the dominant power, and they in turn ruled the country until 1918. Part of the original state of Hungary is now the western section of Romania and the southern section of Czechoslovakia — so today the shrunken territory now has only a population of about three million. It is natural for peasants to sustain their own customs and traditional dance styles of the land of their birth, and this is particularly true of the Magyars (Hungarians), who have kept their music and dance — with its very individualistic quality — intact in spite of the influence of the invading forces of the Tartars, Turks and Austrians. Traditional folk-dance is therefore much more of a regional nature than a political interpretation. The Magyars too are a very colourful race, their love of decoration is manifested in the elaboration of the rhythmic quality of their music, the costume with its accomplished embroidery and even in the painted walls and furniture of their houses.

The greater part of the country is flat, the only mountainous area is in the south-east — the Transylvania region, which is now part of Romania.

The great plains are basically agricultural, and wheat-growing is considerable and of world-wide importance as so much of it is exported. Because of the work associated with farming and the cattle and sheep being so numerous, horse-riding is the national pursuit of the countryfolk.

Music

The orchestras of Hungary are world-famous and consist of strings and the *cymbalom*.

The *cymbalom* is a flat instrument with metal strings, large ones standing on four legs, placed on a table to be played, or on a man's knee when a strap round his neck keeps it in position. It belongs to the dulcimer class, but makes a very strident sound as the strings are struck with a hammer rather than plucked with a plectrum.

Most of the music is in 2/4 or 4/4 time, but often in uneven and short phrases and many changes of tempo, nearly always finishing fast. Because of the quality of the *cymbalom* the beat is very strongly accented, sometimes syncopated and with repeated examples of the "snap".

Ancient instruments such as horns, flutes and a special bag-pipe called a *duda* are rarely found today, but their influence is shown in the melodic line of many of the popular folk-tunes heard now.

Gypsy orchestras frequently accompany the dancers at village festivals and their music is based on that of the country of their adoption (as in Spain, Romania, Italy etc.) but it always has a more romantic and flamboyant quality and this is particularly so in Hungary. The Magyar musician produces music with a harsher tone. Its hard and often sad feeling reflecting the resistant and often war-like nature of the peasant against the invaders of his land, and the troubled history and sufferings of his people.

Many famous composers have immortalised their folk music, such as Liszt, Brahms, Dvòrak, Dohnány, Kodály and Bartók, etc.

Costumes

The Hungarian costumes are amongst the most beautiful and elaborate in Europe and show a very individual style. The one and half centuries of Turkish occupation which the Hungarians fiercely resisted, had little or no influence on their traditions or costumes. The Hungarian pride and strength of character is shown in the very distinctive styles.

Women's skirts are short, very full and are either finely pleated or gathered. Made from linen or cotton they can be plain or floral patterned. A feature of the costumes are the many white petticoats which can number eight, nine or more. These are frequently starched and in some regions are worn over a pad which gives a very bulky outline to the hips. petticoats were considered a sign of wealth and a girl wearing several was always sought after by the young men. Blouses range from a simple style to ones with full gathered, short sleeves which in some regions are starched to make them stick out. Aprons are colourful, sometimes beautifully embroidered as in the central regions, or white and very full as in the North. In the South they are floral, braided and edged with fringe. Shawls and bodices also show a wide range of designs, many being very elaborate and beautifully embroidered. Many of the dances have quick turning movements so generally the head-dresses are small and neat or the young girls have their hair in a plait down the back. The knee length full skirts, together with the numerous petticoats restrict the movement in the upper leg but allow for freedom from the knee downwards and also for twisting movements in the hips as in the side and close of the basic *Czardas* step. Boots or heeled shoes also give weight and depth to the movement.

The men's costumes are based on two styles, either black, tight fitting trousers tucked into black boots, or the white linen, very full divided skirt or trousers called *gatya*. Black waistcoats with silver buttons, white skirts, some with full, loose sleeves, and black boots are worn with both styles. In Matyo region in the north-east, elaborately decorated aprons are worn over the *gatya*, whilst in Szany in the west, the aprons are plain, and in the south, striped. Hats are small, round crowned (not unlike an English bowler) or like an American *Homberg*.

The shepherds and horsemen of the Hortobágy region of the Great Plain wear a *gatya* which is dyed dark blue, a practical colour in a dusty area and also considered lucky. In winter, a large white or saffron coloured felt coat or *szür* is worn like a cloak. Lined with sheepskin they are beautifully decorated with braid and applique work.

Traditional Dances and Style

Because of the quality of the music and strong type of foot-wear, the movement is obviously going to be very hard and forceful — brittle and often syncopated. The emphasis has a downward action on the beat, and is interpreted with clicking of the heels together; and with the horse-riders (either military or herdsmen — called *csikós*) the clips and rattle of the spurs add an exciting sound. The men too emphasise the rhythm by hitting their boots with their hands in many variations of arm lines which give an added interest and often decorative effect.

There are three main types of dancing in Hungary: (1) the peasant or regional style, which is being considered here, (2) the *Palotas* or semi-professional style, once performed in the palaces and houses of the aristocracy—now seen in the theatre, (3) the gypsy style, the dancers performing in bare feet and with exaggerated body movements.

Couple dances, and circular formations are usual — as well as separate dances for men and women.

For men the military background has influenced so much of the style. The *hajdu* a word derived from *heyduck*, meaning cattle-driver, as far back as the 16th Century (when the Turks were the aggressors) practised various forms of sword dances, either dancing over them — like the Scots, or swinging them up and round their bodies in interesting patterns. This was because the men were always alert and ready to resist the invaders (the swords in these dances today are replaced by sticks. The cattle-herders and shepherds also danced over crossed sticks, axes or crooks. These men originally had to defend their animals against wild boars, and thieves particularly when they had to drive them many miles to market through the solitary countryside.

The recruiting dances, called *verbunk* are still very popular. They were originally danced by a sergeant and a group of soldiers when visiting the villages in order to lure the country lads into the army. When a young man was recruited he was handed a silver coin, and a be-ribboned *shako* was placed on his head. These dances originated when a strong army was needed to resist the Austrian invaders.

Of the many dances for women only, the most famous probably are the ones with pillows. They were originally performed by the bridesmaids at a wedding when the beautifully embroidered pillows (or bolsters) were made as gifts for the bride. Others on that occasion too were performed with a shawl or embroidered quilt. Cooks have a special dance too, carrying their cooking utensils when coins would be thrown into them. Another attractive dance is the *karikazo* with twisting actions from the hips, the purpose being to show off the beautifully pleated skirts as well as the numerous petticoats worn underneath.

Of the couple dances, the *csárdás* is the most significant. The step has a syncopated rhythm (which the Americans call Charleston!); but the sequences vary very much according to the technical skills of the performers. It is a courtship dance which originated when a group of peasants gathered together outside the local inn (*csárda* means inn). Often a handkerchief is used to tease the partner, or to link them together: the man shows off with noisy steps with much hitting of his boots, and the girl flirts, spinning away and towards him, sometimes turning on one foot with the other hooked round her boot (a form of pirouette). The dance usually starts slowly, then increases in speed and excitement as it progresses.

Other interesting dances are those of craftsmen: coopers who use the metal hoops from the barrels, weavers, furriers etc. Bottles too feature frequently — women dance with them on their heads; men place them on the ground and dance in patterns between and over them. In the dances at harvest time, be-ribboned scythes, rakes, branches etc., signify the type of work they do. The Magyars are truly a dancing nation.

Customs

The peasant customs of this country are numerous; but with the pace and sophistication of modern life — too many of these now only exist as children's games — but let us hope they will not be entirely forgotten.

Customs to do with the path of life — birth, marriage, and death; the seasons of the year; and festivals associated with saints days are common to every country — some more than others — Hungary is particularly rich in this field.

Shrove Tuesday is a great time for feasting and merriment before the quiet period of fasting associated with Lent.

When Easter (or *húsvét* meaning eating of meat) arrives, one of the first things a peasant would do would be the burning of *Prince Cibere*. *Cibere*, meaning cabbage soup — one of the prevalent and unpalatable dishes of their Lenten diet! This was symbolised by a crude form of doll made from rags and straw.

On Easter Monday, often called Ducking Monday, the young lads would try to throw pails of water over the girls; if a girl was caught she had to pay him a forfeit, either a special kind of bread roll, a glass of brandy or a painted egg. Painted eggs are found in many other countries in Europe and apart from being decorative (painted either bright red or with intricate patterns of many colours) are symbolic of resurrection. They can also be exchanged between young couples as a sign of their engagement. Another rather amusing idea of courtship is when a young man presents his girl-friend with an apple in which a silver coin is embedded; if she accepts it, then all is well!

May-trees again are another form of courting symbol; a bough of a tree is cut down, then all the lower branches cut off so that only the top remains, then the rest is decorated with ribbons, coloured scarves, bottles of wine and again painted eggs: the boys carry it and set it up outside the house of a marriageable girl. These may-trees are also put outside a church in order to ward off evil and to prevent sickness.

At Whitsuntide roses and peonies are seen everywhere. A popular use of them is the making of the crown of the Whitsun Queen, who was always a small girl aged four or five, dressed in white and carried in procession to the church.

At the summer solstice held on St. Ivan's day many sun-worshipping rituals are found; with the giving of green apples, cherries and other fruits to one's friends.

A wedding naturally is an occasion for merry-making and dancing. The skill of the embroiderers is shown on the pillows and silken bed-covers made for the bride's trousseau, as well as on the colourful costumes worn by the men and women.

The giving of hemp is usual — as it is a sign of fertility and is used to decorate the green branch carried by the guests.

Harvest — always a time of rejoicing (especially if it has been a successful one) and it is called the Feast of Wheat.

At this time the making of bread is very significant when the women model the dough into different shapes, the heart and a cockerel being the most usual. It is also the time of the grape harvest when much drinking of wine, takes place and when it is the season of good-will and fellowship.

December 13th is St. Lucia's day, when many strange customs and superstitions are still found. A four-legged wooden stool is elaborately carved using thirteen pieces, the same number as the date of St. Lucia. The stool also takes thirteen days to make, it being completed on Christmas Day.

Cacklers, groups of boys or young men, take straw or a log of wood and place them on the door-steps of houses, then sing special songs to do with magic and fertility. The mistress of the house then rewards them, puts the straw under the hens in order to encourage them to lay eggs, have chickens and cackle!

So creation of life in its many forms or images is always the fundamental basis for fertility rites.

POLAND

The dances of Poland have a vibrant quality, covering the ground well and using strong ballon.

General Background

Poland is situated in the middle of a large expanse of flat land which stretches from Northern France through the Low Countries, Northern Germany, Poland, Western Russia as far as the Urals and is known as the Great European Plain. The section occupied by Poland has a 300 mile northern coastline onto the Baltic Sea and contains the two major ports of Gdansk (formerly Danzig) and Szczecin. In the north east Poland shares a border with the U.S.S.R., in the west with East Germany (German Democratic Republic) and in the south the high Carpathian Mountains separate the country from Czechoslovakia.

There are six major regions in Poland, each with its own music, dances, songs, costumes and customs. In the centre is Masovia with the present capital of Warsaw. Little Poland with the ancient capital of Cracow is in the east. The oldest region, Great Poland is in the west; Pomerania is on the Baltic Sea: Silesia shares a border with East Germany and the Carpathians in the south. Poland has known many hardships and glories as the country expanded and contracted as its power increased or decreased. In the 16th Century, Poland had absorbed the Ukraine, Byelorussia and Lithuania and had reached its widest limits extending from the Baltic to the Black Sea. It was a period of glory for Poland with the arts and sciences flourishing and Poland's prodigious position much admired. The country being flat and having no natural barriers, apart from the mountains in the south, was vulnerable to attack from the surrounding powerful states. Through a series of wars the land gradually became reduced and by the end of the 17th Century a quarter of the land had been captured. A long War of Succession with Sweden, both royal houses being related, had established a Swedish King on the Polish Throne. From 1795 to 1918 there was no such country as Poland on the map, the land being divided between Germany, Russia and Austria. Due to the partitions of the land, political, religious, and national uprisings in the 18th and 19th Centuries, many Poles emigrated to France, Germany, Sweden and the U.S.A.

Agriculture is of great importance to Poland's economy with over half the land being cultivated, and until the advent of the Second World War 61 per cent of the population gained a living working on the land. With the acquisition of Silesia from Germany after the Second World War, this region has become the great coalmining and industrial area. Less people now work on the farms, although agriculture is still of major importance with rye, potatoes, oats, wheat, barley, and sugar beet being the main crops and large numbers of cattle, pigs and sheep being raised.

Among the outstanding features of the country are the many horses and the numerous birch trees (a quarter of the land is covered with pine and birch forests). The Poles have always been excellent riders, horses being used both in a military capacity and also as transport in the rural areas. There are thousands of small country communities, as well as major cities and towns, but the easiest form of rural communication and travel was by horse.

The Poles have suffered many hardships but they have always retained a strong individuality and self-discipline, together with a secure religious outlook. Catholic by faith, rather than the Eastern Orthodox of their Russian neighbours, they have strong attachments to both their land and religion. The present Pope, Pope John Paul II, formerly the Archbishop of Cracow, Cardinal Karol Wojtyla, on his return visits to his native country, always kneels and kisses the ground. The strong national and religious outlook is counterbalanced by their warmth and passion which is shown in their music, songs and dances.

Music

The music of Poland has an animated quality provided by little village bands consisting of strings (violin, cello and sometimes double bass), wood-wind (various kinds of flutes) and drums.

The phrasing and rhythms are usually quite straightforward apart from the mazurka which is a very special form of 3/4.

The logical way to play a 3/4 is to put the emphasis on the first beat as in a waltz, or in Poland in the soulful melody of the *Kujawiak*; but the mazurka has an equal emphasis on the second beat of the bar, this stress is often preceded by a dotted note which gives it an added strength. However, what is difficult for dancers to achieve is the continuity of movement reflecting the flow in the music: often it is interpreted by "step and hold" instead of using a pressure forward from the knee of the supporting leg and travelling forward. The music is not written with a staccato second beat, it may be a minim when the sound will be sustained, or it may be another note. This rhythm has popularity and significance in ballet and other dance techniques, and was an inspiration to many composers of classical music.

The rhythm of 2/4 is often interpreted in different forms of polka steps, but the *Krakowiak* is a wonderful example of an interpretation of the sound made by the hooves of galloping horses, and the clipping of the boots of the riders accentuated by the spurs. The accented beats in the mazurka and *Krakowiak* rhythm developed from the horse-riding background.

The *Polonaise,* also in 3/4 time, has accented beats, the dancers commencing on the last beat of the preceding bar, 3.1.2, a feature common to many 18th Century court dances; as in the *minuet, gavotte.* In the courts (and in classical ballet) the *Polonaise* was used as a processional dance to show off the elaborate costumes, the music being played in a much slower tempo than when danced by the peasants. Many composers have written inspiring mazurkas: among popular ones are by Scharwenka, Paderewski, Niewiadomski and Borowski. The music of Chopin particularly reflects the national character of this dancing nation.

Costumes

There is a great variety of regional costumes in Poland, those worn in the Carpathian Mountains are very different from those of the Polish low-lands, the forest region of the north or along the Baltic coast.

Basically the women's costume consists of a blouse, full skirt, petticoats, apron, bodice or jacket. These change considerably in design, shape, and colour. Striped material is very popular in the central and western regions and is used for skirts, aprons and bodices. Floral patterned skirts are more typical of the Cracow region.

Unmarried girls wear a variety of elaborate head-dresses which can range from a simple flower, wreath or head-scarf, to ones which incorporate ribbons, beads, stiffened muslin etc. Married women tuck their hair away into neat caps or headscarves. At a "capping" ceremony the brides hair would be cut and a small cap placed on her head to show her newly married status. A tight-fitting, laced up boot (like a skating boot) is worn in many regions. This type of boot restricts the movement in the ankle and foot, and like a skater, develops the use of the knee and thigh which produces the strong ballon quality found in the dance style.

The men are also very fond of stripes, and their trousers show a range varying from very narrow, broad, multi-coloured, or red and white (Poland's national colours), according to the region. Various types of jackets (some having a military influence), waistcoats, and coats are worn with belts which can be narrow, broad, studded with brass or having brass rings hanging from them. Hats and caps are decorated with ribbons or in the Cracow region, peacock feathers (considered lucky only in Poland). A wedding custom found in Kujawy is to balance a glass of wine on the strong flat brim of the hat whilst performing a slow dance. The most popular costume is that from the Cracow region which features the *sukmana* or peasant's coat known all over Poland in different forms and colours, and the square shaped cap, adopted as the traditional cap by the Polish army. Red or black boots are worn according to the region.

In the Carpathians, both men and women wear the flat mocassin type of shoe (*Kierpce*) favoured by most mountain people. The men wear tight white trousers, white capes or fur lined coats and very broad leather belts. The women have flowered skirts and attractive velvet bodices and white blouses. The flexible shoe allows the dancers to develop more elevation and quick footwork.

In most areas the costumes are decorated with various kinds of borders, gathers, tucks, pleats, tape decoration, strings, studs, beads, buttons, lace and embroidery.

Traditional Dances and Style

The Poles have always had a strong tradition of dance which stems from the closely integrated village and agricultural life of the people. Song and dance was the main form of expression and entertainment for the villagers and nearly every occasion was celebrated with songs and dances. Special dances were performed at weddings, to encourage the crops to grow, for a good harvest and at harvest time. The fishermen used to do a special dance around their nets before setting out for their catch. Dances would welcome the different seasons of the year and help to chase away evil spirits. Many of the dances are purely social and are couples dancing together or in sets and patterned formations.

On of the most popular dances is the mazurka which comes from the central part of the country called Masovia. Known throughout Poland, it can be classed as a national dance rather than a regional. There are numerous variations and figures, these being called out by the M.C. or dance leader. The Masovians are considered to be very strong minded and hardworking and this proudness of character is shown in the movements of the dance. The mazurka rhythm became the basis for many dances such as the *Kujawiak, Oberek*, etc., but with very different timings.

From the region of Kujawy (Masovia), comes the *Kujawiak*, an improvised couple dance which has many variations and is danced in a slow, dignified manner expressing the romantic aspect of the Poles. In complete contrast is the quick *Oberek*, a couple dance in which the man does jumps, grand jeteś, knee drops etc., the difference being that the girl acts as his support. All these dances are in 3/4 or 3/8 time signature, a rhythm that is typical of the dances in the central, western and south-western part of the country.

One of the oldest dances known in many regions is the *Chodzony*, a walking processional dance from which the *Polonaise* is derived. Many of the court and theatre dances owe their origin to the peasant dances which became adapted by the dancing masters to suit the various occasions. The *Polonaise* was always danced at the opening of a ball, the most important person present would lead the dancers into patterns of his choice. The peasants still retain their manner of dancing the *Polonaise*, often accompanied by singing.

Another popular dance is the *Krakowiak*, from the Cracow region in Little Poland. Similar to the mazurka, it was of an improvised nature and has many figures and variations. The dances from this southern region, together with those from the east are mainly in a 2/4 rhythm, and show the quicker characteristics of the people in this area.

The *Polka*, a dance originating in Bohemia, is still very popular in the villages, long after it had outgrown its vogue in the ballrooms.

At the end of the 18th and the beginning of the 19th Centuries, dances such as the *Mazurka, Krakowiak, Kujawiak* etc., became very popular in urban and social conditions and in their modified and adapted versions became known throughout the country. Classed as national dances, they underwent further changes by dancing masters who introduced certain theatrical movements especially when they were performed in the theatre. The interesting rhythms and music made the Polish dances very popular and they soon spread into many of the European courts. The famous Romantic ballerinas such as Fanny Elssler, Fanny Cerrito and Marie Taglioni also presented to a wide public solo dances based on Polish steps and rhythms. The influence of Polish dances is also found in Sweden due to Poland being occupied for a long time by Swedish armies during the 17th Century War of Succession.

The dances from the Tatra mountains are completely different from those of the rest of Poland and in common with all mountain people they have a lively, upward quality and cover very little ground. Many of the mountain dances are for men only and contain energetic jumps, quick footwork and show the spectacular use of axes.

The flatness of the land, the strong military traditions of the Polish people and the love of riding have all added to the general style. The dances cover the ground (in a similar fashion to those of the Ukraine, Russia etc.) with strong well held proud backs, clips, breaks and actions of horse riding. The pressure of the knee used so much in riding contributes to the "ballon" action produced as the dancers skim across the ground.

Customs

Poland, with its strong agricultural and rural background has many customs connected with the seasons, the land and the propagation of the crops. The name Poland derives from the early settlers called Polanie, meaning the "people of the fields" (or plain).

At one time the sowing of the first seeds was a very solemn occasion when the farmer would dress in his festive attire to undertake this important task. Easter is one of the most important times in Poland as it also celebrates the beginning of a new year with winter's death and the return of spring. A straw image called *Marzanna* (the goddess of death and winter) is made, carried through the village and is burnt or drowned. In common with many other countries, beautiful painted eggs are made and a girl will present one to her boyfriend as a special token of affection. On Easter Sunday, eggs are taken to the church to be blessed and then rolled along the borders of the field to protect the crops from thunder and bad weather. Blessed eggs rubbed on the foreheads of any sick animals helped them to recover. The custom of throwing water over each other is found in many East European countries, in Poland the boys may do this to the girls on Easter Monday, but the girls have the privilege of returning the attack anytime until Whit Sunday. On Palm Sunday or Flower Sunday, sprigs of pussy willow or pine branches are taken to the Church to be blessed and then placed in the house as protection during the coming year. On this day young children are sometimes lightly beaten with a willow twig, the children representing the new crops, the beating to induce good, healthy growth. In some parts of Poland friends and neighbours would strike each other with willow twigs to commemorate the scourging Christ received on the way to his crucifixion. From Palm Sunday to Easter the houses are swept and scrubbed whilst the men clean the stables and barns. Real flowers, decorated sticks made from dried flowers, or a tree made from paper, decorate the inside of the houses, a reminder of the awakening of nature.

On Easter Sunday a candle is taken to church and the bearer (usually the housewife) returns with it alight, the flame being used to light the fire on the newly prepared and clean hearth, so heralding a new year. On Easter Monday, girls decorate a branch with ribbons and flowers, known as a *Gaik* or *Gaj*, this is to encourage a successful year.

The Polish people have always had a great love for their farm animals and especially their horses (there are over 100 proverbs which mention a horse). At carnival and Shrovetide festivals, masks are made representing horses, goats and roosters. In many countries St. George is a very popular saint and his day celebrated in different ways. In Poland he is regarded as the bringer of rain and guardian of spring vegetation and animals.

On Mayday, a decorated maypole is placed by the local village boys outside the house of the most marriageable girl. On St. John's Eve, girls make wreaths which are thrown into a river or stream to predict marriage; a custom also found in the Ukraine and other countries. If the wreath sinks or gets stuck then the owner will have to wait for another year. The local boys will try to catch one of the floating wreathes and then claim the owner for his girlfriend.

At harvest time the last sheaf to be cut was made into a beautiful decorated wreath or a smaller one which would be blessed and worn by a specially chosen village girl. Girls also made harvest dolls shaped like a man with which they dance.

After Easter, Christmas is the next important event, the house and the Christmas Tree being decorated with paper cut-outs and decorations. In the four corners of the room a sheaf of the four principal grains, wheat, rye, oats and barley are placed. Hay is spread on the floor and under the tablecloth to remind the household of the stable and manger of Christ's birth. A Christmas manger or *Szopka* is made and carried from house to house, a custom found all over the country. The manger is made in the shape of a church with twin spires.

Peacocks feathers are much admired in Poland and are considered a sign of good luck, a feather being worn in the men's caps. Peacocks were thought to have been brought to Poland in the 16th Century when the Italian Princess Sforza married King Zygmunt I.

SWITZERLAND

The dances have rather a restrained quality and reflect the styles of either Germany, France or Italy according to the region.

General Background

Switzerland is a small country situated in central Europe and surrounded by France, Germany, Austria and Italy. It is a unique country as four languages are spoken. German is the main language and is found in the central and eastern regions. French is spoken in the west around Geneva and Neuchatel, and Italian is the language in the Ticino, south of the Alps. Romansch, a derivation of Latin is spoken only by the inhabitants of the Canton of Graubunden in the south east. Two or more languages are taught at schools and this multilingual ability has made Switzerland an international centre.

Switzerland is scenically one of Europes' most beautiful countries. The high Alps and mountain ranges, numerous lakes, fertile valley and picturesque towns and villages can hardly be surpassed. Although not large in size, it is a land of contrasts with thick snow in the winter and beautiful wild flowers and green valleys in the spring and summer.

Divided into twenty five Cantons, each canton is a miniature state in its own right. Originally there were only three small states, Uri, Unterwalden and Schwyz: from the latter came the name Switzerland. In 1291 these three states united in order to defend their liberty against the Hapsburgs. This union was the beginning of the Confederation which eventually became the Federal State of Switzerland in 1848. Over the centuries of wars and invasions, political boundaries changed and new cantons were added so creating four national languages with four different, although interchanging, cultural influences.

The Swiss have a reputation for cleanliness, punctuality, reliability and neutrality. They are well known as craftsmen (clocks and watches in particular), the country having little mineral or agricultural wealth. Banking, insurance and tourism have over the years made Switzerland the important economic centre of Europe.

Music

As Switzerland is populated by four different ethnic groups, the folk music is as varied as the language they speak in their homes in the four different regions.

In all districts today the accordion is the instrument most likely to be heard accompanying the dancers, its popularity is chiefly due to the fact that it is easily conveyed from place to place and its sound carries so well out of doors.

Before the advent of the accordion (it was invented about 150 years ago), village bands accompanied the dancers; but they are still very popular today. The band may consist of a variety of stringed instruments: violins, celli, double bass: different kinds of wood-wind, sometimes a dulcimer and always drums.

The French speaking people in the west still retain the light quality in their music reflecting the precise sound of their speech. The musical phrases are usually even, the rhythms lively often in 2/4 or 6/8 time and small intervals in the melodic line.

German — the language spoken in the central and eastern part of the country isn't so strongly accented or as powerful as that which is heard in Germany (but very much stronger than the French). The Landler style in 3/4 and the resonant 4/4 time being the most popular.

The Italian language has a romantic and ringing quality, and the music is varied in rhythms; but with clearly accented beats.

The minority group known as Romansch who inhabit the south-eastern district also have a Latin root to their language; but their music has a serene and quieter approach with frequent changes of time signatures and in level phrases.

Yodelling is always associated with the Alpine regions: it was used originally to call the cattle. The Yodeller makes abrupt intervals with his voice (often a complete octave), this has had an effect on their characteristic movement and music.

Costumes

Swiss costumes, especially those of the women, are amongst the most beautiful and decorative to be found in Europe, the designs and embroideries reflecting the colourful wild flowers and spectacular scenery. The costumes are also very individual and show the influence of the neighbouring countries as well as having a definite style of their own.

In the 17th and 18th centuries Switzerland was renowned for her silks, ribbons, braids, lace and embroideries and these were incorporated by the peasants into their costumes.

The French influence is shown in the use of pastel colours for dresses and aprons, with stripes and floral prints being used for bodices and skirts. Small lace or fringed shawls are very popular and the caps and bonnets very neat. Flat, yellow straw hats and winged black lace headdresses are also very characteristic.

The costumes of the German speaking regions lack the simplicity of the French: colours tend to be darker, relieved by bright coloured aprons. The bodices are similar to those worn in the Black Forest, and are decorated with silver chains, buttons and rosettes. Hats in this region are small, often worn on the back of the head or tied on with ribbons.

The Italians love of colour is shown in the costumes from this region with bright skirts, aprons, shawls, headscarves and bodices, only the blouses, which are white, giving a more sober touch.

On the Austrian border and in the Romansch-speaking region, skirts are accordion pleated in red, green, blue, yellow and black. Bodices and blouses are more elaborate. The headdress of black net made like two butterfly wings comes from this region. Firm shoes are worn in most cantons.

By comparison the mens costumes are much more sober apart from the colourful costume worn by the herdsman in the eastern region, with his yellow breeches and red jacket. The basic costume found in most regions is a smock or jacket worn with long dark trousers and strong shoes.

Traditional Dances and Style

The most popular form of dance to be found in Switzerland is the couple dance. Several old circle dances still remain especially in the area around Gruyeres and these are based on the old medieval *Carole* or *Branle* (known to the English as Brawls). During the Reformation in Europe and especially in Switzerland with its strong links with Calvin, dancing was not encouraged and many of the song-dances became forgotten and lost. Several do remain such as *Le Mariadzo, A Moleson*, etc. (all from the Gruyere region) and although they have changed considerably over the centuries it is still possible to detect their basic origin.

The dances of Switzerland are not complicated and many of the couple dances owe their origin to the old fashioned ballroom dances popular in the 19th Century and which are found in Scandinavia and Western Europe.

Similar to the music and costumes, the dances show the influence of styles of the neighbouring countries but still retain an individual interpretation according to the region, different steps, holds and patterns being introduced.

In the German speaking cantons there are many Landler type of couple dances which are similar to those found in Austria and Germany, but danced with a less boisterous approach, apart from the hill farmers of Toggenburg and Appenzell.

The French dances in the west have a neat approach but are not quite as precise or accented as when danced in France. The dances from the Italian cantons are both flowing and vigorous in style.

There are many dances in the popular Quadrille formation, several with figures that are reminiscent of English Country Dances which during the

17th and 18th Centuries were popular in Europe, especially in the French courts. Dances such as *Polka Piquee, Valse Frappee, Polka Baviere, La Valse, Scottish* (or *Schottische*) *Joyeuse*, etc. show in their names the countries of origin. Very popular are dances which begin in a polka, waltz or mazurka, and then change the rhythm or time signature for a quick end returning to the slow section on the repetition.

Customs

The division of the country leads to a variety of different customs, many have the same traditional theme and are found in the surrounding countries but change slightly in name, concept and time according to the canton, religion and character of the local people.

New Year is welcomed in most cantons with the ringing of handbells and by masked figures wearing large bells on their costumes. In the eastern cantons it is called *Silvesterklause* after St. Nicholas whose status as a saint was diminished at the time of the Reformation and his appearance postponed until the New Year.

Widespread is the custom of "The Three Kings and their Star" at Epiphany, 6th January, when dressed in white and followed by a lighted star four boys travel through the various villages. In the canton Valais the boys ride on beautifully carved hobby horses. In February, bonfires are made on which are burnt large straw men (representing winter), a reminder that spring is imminent.

Spring is a time for many carnivals at which people wear masks, bonfires made and large wheels of fire are thrown from the mountain sides down into the valleys. In the Italian Canton of Ticino, free risotto is served to everyone at the carnival which is eaten heartily before Lent begins.

On the third Sunday before Easter, little wooden rafts bearing candles are placed on some rivers or streams, a custom linked with the traditions of fire and the sun.

In the Roman Catholic areas of the east and central regions, palms are blessed (usually sprigs of holly or branches of evergreen) and then kept to protect farms and pastures. Maypoles are erected on the first Sunday of May and is an occasion for songs and dances around them. Children make and carry wooden frames which they have decorated with flowers and leaves.

The cattle being taken up to their summer pastures is a colourful event. The procession is led by the decorated "queen" cow with her huge bell and followed by the rest of the herd, the herdsmen and the carts carrying the carved wooden utensils needed for their stay on the mountain. The return in the autumn is also a great time for rejoicing.

In mid-summer, the cattle owners visit the herdsmen for a mountain fete during which displays of flag waving, blowing the alphorn, dancing and wrestling takes place. The "queen" cow is specially garlanded and decorated for the event.

In the autumn, mainly in the mountain areas, large round cheeses are distributed, whilst in the wine growing regions, the grape harvest is cele-brated.

In November, to ward off the impending winter and darkness, children carve and make a hollow in large turnips into which is placed a lighted candle, these are then carried round the village streets.

In Berne, an Onion Market is held every November in gratitude for the help given in 1405 when the city caught fire. All kinds of fruit, vegetables and especially onions are sold.

In common with other countries, St. Nicholas arrives on December 6th and in Central Switzerland is greeted in the streets with big noisy processions. Children leave their shoes by the chimney or doorstep for them to be filled with gingerbread and nuts. Sometimes if St. Nicholas is in a hurry the gifts would be thrown in through the window.

AUSTRIA

The Austrians dance with a strong lilting quality reflecting the mountainous landscape and popular rhythm of the Landler.

General Background

Austria is situated in the centre of Europe surrounded by West Germany, Switzerland, Italy, Yugoslavia, Hungary and Czechoslovakia. During the very powerful Hapsburg rule, known as the Austro-Hungarian Empire, most of these neighbouring countries became part of Austria's large and expansive empire.

The capital, Vienna, situated midway between London and Istanbul, Berlin and Rome, Paris and Bucharest, became both politically and geographically the centre of Europe and the Austrian Empire. The country and the capital became a meeting place for many different cultures and people. In Vienna many shops still bear Magyar, Slovenian, Polish, Italian and German names.

The country however has experienced a long and colourful history, often with many hardships. In the 17th Century, the powerful Turkish Ottoman Empire swept through the Balkan countries and Hungary as far as Vienna, but were eventually driven back.

During the Thirty Years War, even Swedish troops occupied part of Austria. It was only after the First World War in 1918 that the Hapsburg Empire finally collapsed and Bohemia, Moravia and Slovakia became Czechoslovakia; Croatia and Slovenia were combined with Serbia, Bosnia etc., to form Yugoslavia; the South Tyrol was given to Italy and Hungary became a republic.

Austria is now no bigger than Ireland, the south and west is mainly mountainous whilst the northern regions of Upper and Lower Austria are fairly flat. The Danube flows across this area, through Vienna and continues on its long journey across Europe. The country is divided into nine states or lander and nearly one-third of the population work on the land, supplying more than three-quarters of the nation's food. The Austrians also make large quantities of wine and over 30,000 acres of land are devoted to vineyards. It was the Romans who introduced viticulture to Austria during their occupation of the capital. Roman soldiers were allowed by regulation two glasses of wine a day, the wine having to be transported with great difficulty and expense from Italy. Vines therefore were planted on the hills around what is now Vienna and have flourished there ever since.

The Austrians are very religious and have a strong Catholic faith. By the roadsides, especially in the Tyrol, carved wooden calvary or crucifixions are placed, protected from the weather by a little roof. In Carinthia and other regions a religious picture is suspended from a pillar.

The Austrians are a cheerful, optimistic and friendly nation, with a great love of life and music, all of which is reflected in their outlook, customs and dances.

Music

With cities like Vienna, and Salzburg and their international reputation in the musical world, the people themselves give music first priority, and each village has its own little band.

In olden times, the mouth organ and zither were the usual instruments to be found. The accordion has taken precedence today (as in many other countries); but it is an Austrian by the name of Damien — a native of Vienna, who invented it in 1829. When the accordion is part of a band it is supported by stringed instruments (violins and double bass) and wood-wind (clarinets or flutes).

The music has a lovely rhythmic swing to it, the majority of the folk-tunes begin in 3/4 time—what they call Landler, and from which the waltz originates.

Large intervals in the melody occur — often as much as an octave, a fact which encourages strong elevation in movement as well as reflecting the art of yodelling.

The polka in 2/4 time is also very popular and found in every district.

People who live in mountainous regions have to move "up and down" all the time and it is true that in every European country that their dances are executed with elevated steps.

The harmony is fairly simple, and the music is usually in regular phrases.

Composers who have been inspired by these lively rhythms are numerous — among the most famous are Beethoven, Mozart, Schumann, Schubert and Strauss.

Costume

Each of the nine states has its own style of costumes with many differences between working, holiday and ceremonial designs. In some of the more isolated mountain regions the costumes have remained unchanged from any outside influences.

When Austria lost her empire, a strong nationalist feeling developed with a revival of peasant costumes and dances and the very popular *dirndl* dress was created for women. Basically it is a full skirt, a bodice of either wool, cotton or velvet, which is laced or buttoned up with silver buttons. Underneath the bodice is a white blouse, and plain or coloured cotton aprons are worn for weekdays, a silk one being used on Sundays. The *dirndl* differs in colours, materials, designs and can be simple or elaborate. It is the basic costume worn everywhere in preference to the more elaborate regional dresses which are only seen on special occasions.

Skirts in all the states are full, those in Burgenland, in the east and now part of Hungary, are very full and show the influence of this country. In Carinthia they are pleated, and in other regions gathered. A great many of the dances involve turning movements so several petticoats are worn. The Catholic Church did not forbid dancing but it did insist on modesty of dress.

Various types of felt hats are found in many regions. White or coloured stockings worn with strong shoes complete the costume.

The most popular costume for men is the leather shorts or breeches (*Lederhosen*). Originally worn only by the hunters in the Styria region, it was adopted by Archduke Johann (who lived in Styria, married a commoner and liked to dress like the people of this region) and later by his grandnephew, Emperor Francis Joseph I. This very practical garment was consequently worn by the Emperor's entourage, copied by everyone and evolved into Austria's national costume. *Lederhosen* can have various forms of decoration on the trouser flaps, pockets and braces, and is worn with a white shirt, different styles of waistcoats or jackets. Felt hats are very popular, usually with the feathers of the mountain bird or a chamois brush fixed into the side. The leather shorts also enabled the men to beat out the *Schuhplattler* rhythms. White socks and black shoes are also worn. There are many different regional costumes which are now worn on special occasions or festivities.

Traditional Dances and Style

The most popular and widely known Austrian dance is the *Schuhplattler*. Originally it began as a couple dance with the boy hitting his thighs and shoes, showing off to his partner and expressing vitality and exuberance. From one couple it gradually developed into several with the men improvising in the middle of a circle while their partners danced admiringly on the outside. Danced now at all folklore occasions it has become very elaborate, the men hissing and clucking to represent the *capercailzie* or black-cock, the well known mountain bird.

Dance, like music, has always been a way of life for the Austrians. Many of the mountain villages and towns are isolated and dance is an important part of their rural and social existence. Couple dances tend to predominate rather than pattern dances, possibly due to the confined space of the mountain regions. During the spring and summer months people are busy on the land, it is mainly at the harvest and winter times that dancing takes place. As in other countries with similar climates, dancing is mainly indoors, especially in the winter, the accent being on turning movements rather than complicated steps. Unique to many of the couple dances are the intricate arm movements and positions which are combined with turning actions and which give to the Austrian dances a very distinct style; a good example is the *Zillertaler Landler*. The Austrians' cheerful approach to life no doubt helped to develop the often amusing arm actions and movements.

In most countries there has been an interchange between the court and peasant dances but perhaps no dance has had such a success as the *Landler* from which derives the present day waltz. At the end of the 18th Century, barges travelling on the Danube from Upper Austria to Vienna would carry with them a group of musicians. The bands would stop at various places along the river and play at the local inns and fairs to earn enough money to take back with them on the return journey. The bright and tuneful *Landler* melodies and dances soon became very popular and adaptations of the dances soon found their way into the ballrooms. The arm movements and twists were found to be too complicated and only the final waltz sequence was retained. Already popular in Vienna, the dance was officially introduced at the Congress of Vienna in 1815 and from that date has been danced continually (with certain changes) in ballrooms throughout the world. Apart from the waltz there are also dances performed by the woodcutters, the miners and the bakers. The *Bandtanz* is a popular maypole dance but performed at weddings rather than at springtime. From the salt mines near Saltzburg the workers executed a Sword Dance and from Carinthia the iron-ore workers dance with hoops. In many areas garlanded hoops are used in dances and processions.

The Austrian style not only shows their friendly and lively nature but also reflects the Italian's love of music, the Hungarian's talent for dancing and the Slav mysticism which is so blended into their background.

Customs

Many of the customs are also popular in the neighbouring countries but often with slight variations. The seclusion of some of the Alpine villages also resulted in several unique customs and festivals developing.

Christmas is one of the most important events of the year and preparations begin early. On 4th December, St. Barbara's Day, twigs, ideally from cherry trees, are collected and put in the house to blossom. If they bloom at Christmas it means good luck and a successful harvest. Often, small pieces of paper with numbers on them are rolled round the twigs and are only unwrapped if the twig blossoms, a present awaits those who have the corresponding number.

On the eve of St. Nicholas, 6th December, *Nikolo* or St. Nicholas (who is dressed like a bishop) brings the presents, or places them in the boots or shoes left overnight outside the door or window. As in Germany an Advent wreath (*Adventkranz*) is made of fir twigs and candles. Christmas trees are decorated on Christmas Eve in a locked room and only when they are completed are the children allowed in. Some children believe that it is the Christ Child or St. Nicholas who has decorated the tree and that the tinsel is part of the angels' hair which got caught on the branches as they flew away once it was completed. A crib is also an important part of the Christmas decorations and amongst the many carols sung "Silent Night, Holy Night" (*Stille Nacht, Heilige Nacht*) is a particular favourite. The composer of this carol, Franz Gruber, lived all his life at Hallien, near Salzburg.

New Year is welcomed as in most countries with bell ringing, and also with trumpet and trombone fanfares played from the church towers.

Epiphany, 6th January, is the time when boys dress up as the Three Kings or Wise Men, and go through the villages singing carols and collecting money for charity. The Kings are preceded by a boy carrying a large star on a pole, the event commemorating the visit of the Wise Men to the baby Jesus.

Spring and Easter are both greeted with bonfires, sometimes called "March Fires" or "Magic Sun". Straw effigies of winter are burnt or filled with gunpowder and blown up. On Palm Sunday bunches of catkins or pussy willow are blessed and then kept as a safeguard against storms and illness. In some regions branches of pine, willow, flowers, ribbons and apples are fastened to the top of a pole. After the pole has been blessed it is placed in the centre of a field to encourage the crops to grow.

Easter Day has all the usual "egg games" and hunting for eggs hidden by the Easter Bunny. To wash in water collected before sunrise on Easter Day ensures beauty and if the water is sprinkled over the fields the crops will be good.

A tall Maypole is erected in most villages and the local boys take it in turns to climb to the top to collect a present that is hidden there.

Corpus Christi Day is one of the most beautiful Autumn festivals when all the houses are decorated with flowers. Children also wear garlands of flowers for the various Church processions. At Hallstatt and Traunkirchen, due to lack of space, the services are held from decorated boats on the lake. This day is also celebrated by the farmers who carry green branches representing sabres; the event commemorating the victory over the Swedish invaders.

The Austrians' close connection with the land results in many agricultural customs. At harvest time the first stalks to be cut are made into a cross and the last into a wreath. There is an old saying "everything that grows tall should be planted when the moon is waxing, and everything beneath the ground when it is waning".

At the village of Thaur, a life-sized, carved wooden donkey is carried through the fields followed by children carrying poles decorated with ivy, *pretzels* and apples (an old harvest relic from the Celtic or Roman occupation). At the wine harvest, clusters of grapes are made into one large bunch and taken to the Church to be blessed and a prayer of thanksgiving said for the good harvest.

The return of the cattle from the summer pastures (as in Switzerland) is greeted with great excitement, and special cakes and biscuits are made by the women to welcome the herdsmen. One charming custom is held on Midsummer Night in Lower Austria when eggshells are filled with lighted candles and floated on the Danube, the whole river becoming a mass of tiny lights.

CZECHOSLOVAKIA

The Czech dancing has a lively, turning quality which varies in its downward emphasis and style from east to west.

General Background

Geographically Czechoslovakia is in the centre of Europe, with the famous city of Prague as its capital.

Czcechoslovakia is composed of three regions, Bohemia, Moravia and Slovakia and was once part of a larger area known as the Moravian Empire. The country came under Austrian domination during the expansion of that Empire, but finally regained its freedom in 1918, becoming known as the Czechoslovakian Republic.

A country with no coastline, it has been greatly influenced by its neighbours. To the north there is a long frontier with Poland, and on the eastern side a short border with the U.S.S.R. A large section of Hungary borders the south-eastern region, then with Austria due south, and Western Germany in the south-west and Eastern Germany in the north-west.

Due to the proximity of the surrounding countries, Czechoslovakia has had a complicated and significant history of wars: Germany, Austria, Hungary and Poland having influenced the cultural activities in the three different regions.

In the 10th Century their famous Premyslid ruler was Vaclav I, who brought Christianity to the country and who became known as the "Good King Wenceslas" in the well-known Christmas carol. He died tragically at the age of 22 but was destined to become the Patron Saint of Czechoslovakia, with a statue honouring him in the main square in Prague.

From the 14th to 18th Centuries civil wars of opposing religious factions, particularly the Hussites, divided the country. During the Austrian Hapsburg regime and the Thirty Years' War, which was felt throughout much of eastern Europe, over 2,000,000 Czechs emigrated to the U.S.A.

After many hardships and mainly through the efforts of Thomas Garrigue Masaryk, the country finally achieved independence in 1918. Masaryk's father was Slovak and his mother Moravian; his wife American. It was through his work during the First World War and his contacts with President Wilson of the U.S.A. that a treaty was signed with the Hapsburgs and a democratic independent state was created. The country continued to prosper until the rise of Hitler, and in the Second World War the Nazis invaded, wrecking the land and destroying the towns. It was in 1942 that the town of Lidice was completely wiped out and which caused such world-wide horror. Finally, Russia came to the aid of the Czechs and the Germans were driven out. Czechoslovakia is now a communist state.

Bohemia in the west — the most populated of the three states — is separated from Germany and Poland by mountain ranges. This region contains most of the major industries and coal mines and is a source of many important minerals, including the precious uranium deposits used by Marie Curie who discovered radium for the benefit of mankind. Found also is a special kind of clay called *Kaolin* which resulted in the making of the world famous porcelain and glass products. Textiles are also an important product and much excellent cloth is made in Liberce, known as "the Manchester of Bohemia".

Moravia is the middle section of the country, with Brno its capital. This region is famous for textiles, shoes (*Bata*), as well as many engineering works. The Morava River in the east separates Moravia from Slovakia and is one of the largest rivers in the country, eventually flowing into the Danube which terminates in the Black Sea. The famous Moldau River flows from Prague and continues northwards through the middle of Bohemia.

Slovakia, the south-eastern section, is very different from Bohemia and Moravia. The people speak a similar language but are more care-free in their general approach to life. Bratislava is the capital and is only 20 miles away across the border from Vienna. This region as a whole is much more rural than the rest of the country; therefore more interesting in its folklore and customs. Due to the influence of the Hungarians and Ukrainians, the population is a mixture of these races and their dances and music have similar qualities and styles.

Music

The music of this country is very lively and most stimulating with its unexpected changes and variety in rhythm and tempi.

Major keys are more usual in the western regions and minor in the east. The interval of a rising 4th is frequently heard in the melodic line.

The most common instruments in olden times were the lyre and a hurdy-gurdy. A type of bag-pipe is found everywhere, and further east the music of the village bands becomes more intricate with the use of violins, clarinets and double basses. In parts of Slovakia the *cymbalom* is found, due to its close proximity with Hungary, with the result of a strongly accented quality in the music.

The composer Smetana was born in the Bohemia-Moravia highlands in 1824 and did much to popularise his country's music; many of his operas are based on folk themes, especially the well-known "Bartered Bride". For many years this famous musician (and skilled violinist) ran a music academy in Sweden, then at the age of 37 returned to his own country and created many works until his tragic death at the age of 60.

Dvorak and Janacek are two other famous composers of the 19th Century who wrote works based on Czech folk-themes. Martinu, a Twentieth Century composer who lived most of his life in France, Switzerland and the U.S.A., still wrote with a truly national flavour. His music portrays his love of his native country and this is very evident in his settings of folk-music, cantatas and ballet music.

The choreographer and dancer requires to study Czech music with care in order to be aware of the cross-accents, changes in time-signatures and uneven phrases that occur so frequently.

Costume

The costumes of Czechoslovakia can be divided into two basic types — those of the lowlands and those of the mountain regions. Within these categories there are many different local variations.

Bohemia's cultural contact with Austria and Bavaria is reflected in the costumes which have strong western influences. The women's skirts are full and often pleated and worn with several petticoats. The pleats used to be made by wetting the material, pressing in the pleats, tying a band round them and then hanging them up to dry. The women are very proud of their pleated skirts and petticoats and show these off by making swift turning movements when dancing. The bodices are tight, firm and worn over white blouses. Bonnet type headdresses are small, round and highly decorated with ribbons or lace; frequently with a bow at the back. Alternatively there are gathered ribbons and headscarves, known as the *satek*, for married women. A firm shoe is the footwear with the lowland type of costume.

The men have either breeches or tight trousers tucked into boots; different styles of waistcoats and jackets, wide-brimmed hats or fur caps.

In the regions near the Hungarian border, the basic outline remains the same but the blouse sleeves become more exaggerated and decorated, skirts and aprons covered with more embroidery and black boots or shoes are worn. The men's costume is also more elaborate with braiding on the tight black or dark trousers, embroidered shirts, decorated waistcoats, boots and black hats with rolled brims, decorated with bunches of flowers and white feathers. The feathers are difficult to find and there is great competition among the men to obtain them. The wearing of a feather is a sign of manhood but once the man is married, the feather is put away. A man will often tuck into his belt or trouser pocket an embroidered handkerchief which has been made and presented to him by his girl-friend.

The type of costume worn in the mountain regions has a strong resemblance to that of their Polish neighbours. The style is based on plain or floral patterned skirts; the blouses are simple with very little embroidery, fewer petticoats are worn and like all mountain people, soft leather mocassins or *kirpce/gripcas* are worn. The men have tight, white felt trousers, braided or embroidered down the front, a wide leather belt with brass studs and buckles, a simple wide-sleeved shirt, soft *gripcas*, a large, wide-brimmed black felt hat, or sometimes a close fitting one.

Ribbons are very popular in Czechoslovakia and are used to decorate costumes, hats etc. Men will often wear a cluster of them in their buttonholes, a gift from their girl-friends. In Moravia the bride on her wedding day will present to the groom a bunch of ribbons. If the ribbons are very long it is a sign that she is fairly wealthy with a good dowry, and if the groom trips over them, this is considered very lucky.

In the regions where boots are worn, the dancers have more emphasis into the ground, stamps and heel clicks are introduced and the men perform *capas*, the slapping of boots, which contrast with the less accented movement found in the western area. The *gripcas* shoes of the mountain people allow for speed, lightness and elevation.

Traditional Dances and Style

The polka is a dance that is closely associated with Bohemia. It was thought to have been brought to Vienna by a dancing master who happened to see a village girl dancing it. Similar in history to the waltz, it became adapted and developed to suit the ballrooms of Europe, yet was executed in its simple and original style by the peasants. The polka step is performed in nearly every country in Europe, but executed in varying styles according to the music and temperament of the different nations.

In Czechoslovakia the polka has many variations: but a very distinctive quality; the movement has an emphasis into the ground before the elevation (similar to the action of using a spade when digging in the garden).

The *Furiant* is a very popular and lively dance, usually written in 3/4 time; but the dancer frequently using steps in a 2/4 rhythm, thus creating interesting cross-accents. There is also a well-known popular carol heard at Christmas using a *Furiant* melody but sung at a slower tempo with 3 bars of 2/4 and 2 bars of 3/4.

Most of the Czech dances are performed by couples with quick, lively, turning movements and with strongly accented footwork. In common with their Austrian and Hungarian neighbours the girls like to turn to show off their beautifully pleated skirts, petticoats and the lovely embroidered ribbons (worn by both men and girls).

The most ancient form of dance (as in most countries), was circular; but after the 16th Century when the Italians influenced so much of the country's culture, the couple dance was introduced and is the most usual form seen today.

There are many regional dances influenced by the terrain and the proximity of the surrounding countries. In the Tatra Mountains the men's dances show the same strength and elevation as the mountaineers across the border in Poland. The lumber workers in the Slovakian Highlands also dance in a similar style using their axes and executing high jumps associated with mountain people. The shepherds from Wallachia have many dances of an improvised nature during which they rival one another and perform various tricks and games, not unlike the improvised dances found in the U.S.S.R. In the regions near the Hungarian border the *Czardas* type of couple dances are found. The Slovaks adopted this very Hungarian dance but changed it considerably, the music being typically Slavic and the steps and movement very vigorous but freer than the Hungarian version.

There are also many dances which show the various occupations, the blacksmith, the shoe-maker, the sowing and reaping of the harvest. One of the most colourful is the *Makovy Tance* or Poppy Dance, depicting the growth and cultivation of the poppy, the dancers miming the sowing, thinning out, the general growth of the plants and finally picking and eating the seeds.

Customs

Like all European countries, the peasants have special festivals to mark the different seasons of the year. In Czechoslovakia their special carnival takes place just before Lent and is one of the most important events, lasting a whole week. Beginning on what is called "Fat Thursday" (the day on which everything is eaten and finished up before Lent begins) and continuing till Ash Wednesday. Often at this time of the year it is cold with hard frosts, even snow on the ground. The masked dancers mime the action of ploughing (but this is done in the snow, not the earth!). Many disguises are worn by the dancers (rather like the English Morris men) such as the Devil, a Jew, a chimney sweep, a kind of Harlequin and the Baba, a special figure in central Europe and usually interpreted by the local dancing master.

Midsummer or St. John's Day is a time for making bonfires and for jumping over them to ensure that you would not die during the coming year. Herbs collected on this day especially before sunrise, were very beneficial and kept throughout the year. Young men carrying brooms dance round the fire and then plant the signed broom in the fields to make the crops grow. Girls make wreaths of wild flowers, then throw them into the fire — the girl who made the first wreath to burn would be married within the year. Also popular is the custom of throwing the wreath into a river or stream to see if it sinks or floats, thereby foretelling marriage. Another method is to dig into the ground with the heel of the shoe and place a piece of bread in the hole. Next day if the bread was intact then they will be a spinster; if an ant was sitting on it, then she will soon have a sweetheart; if, however, a starling then she will marry a widower.

A village wedding is always a setting for customs and dances, the festivities usually lasting for a whole week. The use of rosemary features very much on these occasions: unmarried girls wear crowns of this herb decorated with white ribbons and the young men always wear a sprig in their buttonholes. Instead of a wedding cake, the bride's mother bakes a large confection of pastry modelled or plaited into interesting shapes; this is then held over the head of the chief guest while everyone dances round her. When the dance ends the cake is cut into pieces and eaten by the company.

The long handled axes found in Slovakia have beautifully decorated, carved or painted handles. These axes which are used in many dances can also be used by two men having a mock fight, or by a man courting a girl when he shows off his strength and agility.

The day preceding Palm Sunday is when the men from the villages go down to the wood to cut branches from the willow trees. The branches are then cleaned and planted in the fields to make sure that the year's harvest will be a good one.

The Wednesday before Easter is known as "the Sad Wednesday" and is the time when people clean and paint their houses. On Good Friday, before it is dawn, young girls go down and wash themselves in a stream to ensure good health and beauty in the coming year. The cleaning or "Ritual of Purification" found in many countries just before Easter is the origin of "spring cleaning".

In common with many countries in Central and Eastern Europe, eggs are decorated at Easter. One of the most popular colours for dyeing eggs is red, in Bohemia Easter was called a "red holiday". Red was considered to be a proud and heroic colour and was also used to deter the evil eye.

On Easter Monday, young men with willow canes go from house to house asking the young girls for presents. With the canes they beat the girls very gently and in return they are given a decorated egg. In some areas boys and girls drench each other with water, an ancient symbol of Spring cleansing ceremonies. In Bohemia on Easter Sunday before the main meal begins all those sitting at the table have to share pieces of hard-boiled eggs and wish each other good luck.

May is an occasion for decorating may-poles; small ones are made by the boys in the village and placed at night outside the houses of the girls they are courting. If the girl likes him, she will accept the gift and next day the boy will take her as his partner to dance round the big may-pole on the village green.

GLOSSARY

Accelerando   Gradually getting quicker.

Adagio   Slow and leisurely.

Air   A tune or melody.

Allegretto   Lively, moderately fast.

Allegro   Brisk, lively and rapid.

Alpenhorn   A primitive wood-wind instrument of Swiss origin.

Anacrusis   The unaccented note (or notes) which precede the first accented beat of a bar or phrase.

Andante   Walking pace, or moving along in a flowing steady tempo.

Augmented 2nd   An interval of three half tones; or a major interval increased by a semi-tone (e.g. Middle C to D sharp).

Bag-pipe   An ancient wind-instrument (of many types) consisting of a leather bag which holds the air; 2 or 3 pipes called drones, and a short pipe with finger holes upon which the tune is played.

Ballon   A bouncing action; the springing movement of a dancer.

Baldricks   Ribbons worn by Morris men, placed over the shoulders and crossed in front of the shirt.

Basket-hold   Dancers in a circle holding the arms in a low V line; joining hands with the next but one, held either in front or behind the body of the adjacent dancer.

Beat   The musical pulse.

Bolero   A lively Spanish dance in triple-time.

Bourree   A lively dance of French origin usually in 4/4 time.

Cantabile   In a singing style.

Carillon   A tune played on bells.

Chanter   The finger-pipe of a bag-pipe on which the melody is played.

Chord   A combination of 3 or more notes played at the same time.

Coda   A "tail". A phrase added at the end of a piece of music in order to emphasise its conclusion.

Compound time   When a beat or pulse is divisible into three (e.g. 6/6 the compound of 2/4 and 9/8 of 3/4 etc.).

Crescendo   A gradual increase in sound.

Cross-accent   A "shifting" of the accent, e.g. if the music is in 3/4 time (the player accenting the first beat) and the dancer executing steps in 2/4 time, or vice-versa, thus ignoring the bar-lines but the beats being of the same value.

Cross-phrase   When the sequence of steps is irregular and does not coincide with the musical phrase e.g. a ten bar sequence of steps to music written in eight bar phrases.

Cross-rhythm   When either the dancer or musician use beats of different value within the bar lines, e.g. if music is in 3/4 time and the dancer performs 2 or 4 steps in the bar.

Diminuendo   Gradually getting quieter.

Dolce   Sweet or soft.

Dotted Note   A dot placed after the written note in the music, thus prolonging its value by a half.

Dulcimer   An ancient stringed instrument: the strings being stretched over a sounding board — struck with hammers, or plucked by the player.

Enchainement   A series or chain of steps linked together.

Emphasis   Stress.

Epaulement   Literally — shouldering — the line of the shoulders in relation to the body. Also the line of the body in relation to the audience.

Forte   Loud and strong.

Glockenspiel   An instrument consisting of a set of bells which are struck with a hammer.

Guitar   An instrument which usually has 6 strings which are plucked with the right hand, and the notes "stopped" on the strings with the left hand.

Harmony   A combination of musical sounds which accompany the melody.

Interval   The distance between one note and another; or the difference in pitch between two sounds.

Landler   A slow waltz.

Largo   Large, broad or stately.

Legato   Smooth or flowing.

Lento   Slow.

Lute   An ancient stringed instrument.

Maestoso   With dignity — or majestically.

Mazurka   A rhythm of Polish origin in 3/4 time, with the emphasis usually occurring on the second beat in the bar.

Measure   Another word for a bar in music.

Opanki or opinci   A type of flat shoe worn in the Balkans.

Pas   A step in a dance sequence.

Phrase   A collection of bars which may be of a long or short duration (a musical sentence).

Piano   Soft or quiet.

Plectrum   A small piece of ivory, horn, quill or metal used for plucking strings.

Rapper   A sword made of pliable wood used by Morris men.

Rubato   A slowing up of the tempo.

Schuhplattler   A dance from the Alpine region in which men perform the "plattler" showing off to the girls. These are beats made by stamps, slapping the thighs and shoes in variations of 3/4 time. The leather shorts (*lederhosen*) heighten the sound of the slaps. Traditionally these sounds imitated the wing-beats made by the black-cock (*capercaillzie*) in the mating season.

Simple time   When each beat or pulse in the music is divided into equal parts e.g. 2/4, 3/4, 4/4.

Snap   A term usually associated with Scottish music; the timing being "Quick-slow". This is usually written as a semi-quaver followed by a dotted quaver: it is also found in Hungarian music; but used in a different manner.

Sporran A type of loose pocket made of leather which is worn over the kilt. Originally it acted as a form of protection as well as being used to carry money, valuables, etc. For ceremonial dress it is made of fur.

Staccato A sharp detached sound by the player. It is indicated by a dot placed over the written note.

Tambourine A drum-like instrument with metal discs attached which make a jingling sound.

Tempo Time, speed — or style of movement.

Vivace Lively and quick.

BIBLIOGRAPHY

North

Icelandic Feasts and Holidays by Arni Bjornsson, Iceland Review, Reykjavik 1980.

The National Costume of Women in Iceland by Elsa E. Gudjonsson, Reykjavik, 1976.

Folk Dancing in Norway by Johan Krogsaeter. Johan Grundt Tanum Forlag, Norway 1968.

Phantoms and Fairies from Norwegian Folklore by Tor Age Bringsvaerd, Norway.

Svenska Folkdanser by Svenska Ungdomsringen for Bugdekultur, Stockholm 1964.

Dances of Sweden by Erik Salven. Max Parrish & Co., London 1949.

Denmark by Nina Nelson. B. T. Batsford Ltd., London 1973.

Dances of Denmark by Poul Lorenzen and Jeepe Jeppesen. Max Parrish & Co., London 1950.

The Netherlands, European Folk Dance Series by Nigel and Margeret Allenby-Jaffe, Folk Dance Enterprises, Skipton 1982.

South

Folk Dances, Costumes & Customs of Italy by Elba Farabegoli Gurzau. Folkraft Press, U.S.A. 1964.

Italy: An Unauthorised Portrait by Franco Ferrarotti. Alitalia 1973.

Fodor's 1982 Guide to Spain. Hodder & Stoughton 1982.

Spanish Dancing by Wingrave and Harrold. Planned Action Ltd. 1972.

Dances of Portugal by Lucile Armstrong. Max Parrish & Co., London 1948.

Portugal by Rodney Gallop. Cambridge 1961.

Portuguese Dances by Pedro Homem De Mello. Lello & Irmao, Porto, Portugal 1962.

East

Folk Traditions in Yugoslavia, by Leposava Zunic-Bas. Isdavacki Zavod, Yugoslavia.

The Companion Guide to Jugoslavia by J. A. Cuddon. Collins, London 1974.

Yugoslavia by Lovett F. Edwards. Batsford, London 1971.

Russian Folklore by Y. M. Sokolov. Folklore Associates, Pennsylvania, U.S.A. 1966.

The Sabres of Paradise by Lesley Blanch. Quartet, London 1978.

The Land and People of Poland by Joan Charnock, Adam and Charles Black, London 1967.

The Poles: How they live and work by Marc E. Heine, David and Charles, Newton Abbot 1976.

Song, Sance and Customs of Peasant Poland by Sula Benet. Dennis Dobson, London 1951.
Dances from Cuiavia by Roderyk Lange. Centre for Dance Studies, Jersey, C.I. 1976.
The Greeks: How they live and work by T. R. B. Dicke. David & Charles, Newton Abbot 1972.
Folk Dances of the Greeks by T & E Petrides. Exposition Press, New York, U.S.A. 1961.
Greek Dances by T. Petrides. Lycabettus Press, Athens, Greece 1975.
Greek Costumes by Ioanna Papantoniou. Athens, Greece 1973.
Dances, Music and Costumes of Bulgaria by Wingrave & Harrold. London 1978.
Bulgarian Folk Dances by R. Katzarova-Kukudova & K. Djenev. Sofia, Bulgaria 1958.
Romania by Peter Latham. Garnstone Press, London 1967.
Dances of Romania by Miron & Carola Grindea. Max Parrish & Co., London 1952.
Folk Costumes, Textiles & Embroideries of Rumania by T. Banateanu. G. Focsa, E. Ionescu, Romania 1958.

West

Dances of Germany by Agnes Fyfe. Max Parrish & Co., London 1951.
German Festivals and Customs by Jennifer M. Russ. Oswald Wolff, London 1982.
The French; How They Live & Work by J. T. Carroll. David & Charles, Newton Abbot 1977.
Dansez la France. Books I & II by Monique Decitre. Editions Dumas, Saint-Etienne, France 1951/1963.
A Guide to French Fetes by E. I. Robson. Methuen & Co. Ltd., London 1930.
The Land of Pardons by Anatole Le Braz. Methuen & Co. Ltd., London 1906.
Folk Music and Dances of Ireland by Brendan Beathnach. Mercier Press, Dublin 1971.
The Year in Ireland by Kevin Danaher. Mercier Press, Dublin 1972.
Dances of England and Wales by Maud Karpeles & Lois Blake. Max Parrish & Co., London 1950.
Dance of Scotland by Jean C. Milligan & C. G. MacLennan. Max Parrish & Co., London 1950.
Rantin' Pipe and Tremblin' String by George S. Emmerson. J. M. Dent & Sons Ltd., London 1971.
The Swinging Sporran by Andrew Campbell & Roddy Martine. Wolfe Ltd., London 1973.
Folklore & Customs of Rural England by Margaret Baker. David & Charles, Newton Abbot 1974.
A Harvest of Festivals by Marian Green. Longman, London 1980.

Origins of Festivals & Feasts by Jean Harrowven. Kaye & Ward, London 1980.

Let's Dance — Country Style by Ronald Smedley & John Tether. Paul Elek Books Ltd., London 1972.

Traditional Britain by Mark Martin. Sidgwick & Jackson, London 1983.

Centre

Czechoslovakia by John Burke. Batsford Ltd., London 1976.

Czechoslovakia by Fodor. Hodder & Stoughton, London 1977.

Traditions and Popular Festivals in Switzerland. Swiss National Tourist Publication.

Folk Dances and Costumes of Switzerland by Wingrave & Harrold. London 1977.

Austria by Virginia Waite. B. T. Batsford, London 1970.

Dances of Austria by Katharina Breuer. Max Parrish & Co., London 1948.

Hungarian Dances by Karoly Viski. Simpkin Marshall Ltd., London 1937.

Hungarian Peasant Customs by Karoly Viski. George Vajna & Co., Budapest 1932.

The Pearly Bouquet by Bela Paulini. George Vajna & Co., Budapest 1937.

General

Musical Instruments Through The Ages by Anthony Bainer. Penguin Books 1961.

Grove Dictionary of Music & Musicians. Macmillan Ltd., London 1980.

The Nature of Dance by Roderyk Lange. Macdonald & Evans Ltd., London 1975.

Easter the World Over by Priscilla Sawyer Lord & D. J. Foley. Chilton Book Co., U.S.A. 1971.

Dictionary of Folklore, Mythology & Legend. New English Library, London 1975.

Easter Eggs by Victor Houart. Souvenir Press, London 1978.

Christmas Customs around the World by Herbert H. Wernecke. Bailey Brothers, Folkestone 1974.

Superstition & the Superstitious by Eric Maple. W. H. Allen, London 1971.

May I have the Pleasure by Belinda Quirey. B.B.C. London 1976.

World History of the Dance by Curt Sachs. Norton & Co. New York, U.S.A. 1963.

European Folk Dance by Joan Lawson. Pitman & Sons Ltd., London 1953.

Folk Costumes of the World by Robert Harrold. Blandford Press, Dorset 1978.

Family of Man Encyclopoedia. Marshall Cavendish Ltd., London 1978.

Magazines

"Viltis" Denver, U.S.A.

Ontario Folk Dancer, Toronto, Canada.